GREAT AMERICAN LIBERALS

GREAT
AMERICAN
LIBERALS

Edited by Gabriel Richard Mason

STARR KING PRESS   BOSTON

Contents

GREAT AMERICAN LIBERALS

Preface

Disraeli, speaking to the House of Commons in 1848, said, "Liberalism is the introduction into the practical business of life of the highest kind — namely politics — of philosophical ideas instead of political principle."

In the same sense, we may say, American liberalism is not a set of principles of any single political party. Nor is it an ideology like communism or fascism. It is, rather, a dynamic power that guides men and women of vision toward a constantly improving society. It is one of the driving forces of America's permanent revolution. Negatively, liberalism is a movement *away* from tyranny, be that tyranny political, social, or economic. Positively, liberalism is a steady movement *toward* the realization of the noble ideals so clearly set forth in our Declaration of Independence by our Founding Fathers. Nor should we ignore the seminal contributions to liberalism made by the great Europeans — men of the stature of Milton, Locke, Spinoza, and the philosophers of the French Enlightenment.

Few will dispute these statements. Unfortunately, there are also too few who are actuated by their implications in our everyday affairs. Too many of us are lulled into complacency by the apparent march of our great technology. Too many of us are not sufficiently sensitive to the fact that it is liberalism throughout our history that has steered our technology toward our vaunted high standard of living and toward successful experimenting with a great federal republic. Too many of us are not sufficiently mindful of the threats that democracy faces from hostile, competing ideolo-

gies — threats not only from the left of which we have fortunately become aware; but also from the right toward
which we are too inactively conciliatory. For all these
reasons a refresher in the history of liberalism in America
— in the highlighting of its accomplishments and of its aspirations — becomes a desirable course for all citizens.

The twelve representative figures discussed in this book
were not chosen for their uniqueness, nor for their influence
in shaping the American mind. The selection was made on
the basis of their cumulative contribution to our social, cultural, and political history. Interestingly enough, as individuals they represent true democratic leadership in the
sense that they merely articulated and, perhaps, gave direction to the countless and nameless people who make up the
American nation.

Great American Liberals owes its existence to the City
College Club, under whose auspices twelve men closely associated with the City College of New York generously
contributed their scholarship to create this book.

                                    Gabriel Richard Mason

I

Tom Paine

Buell G. Gallagher

Buell G. Gallagher, president of the College of the City of New York, was formerly assistant commissioner of the U.S. Office of Education. He has also served as president of Talladega College, in Alabama, and as professor of Christian Ethics at the Pacific School of Religion, Berkeley, California. His books include *American Caste and the Negro College; Color and Conscience: The Irrepressible Conflict;* and *Portrait of a Pilgrim: A Search for the Christian Way in Race Relations.*

Tom Paine

Buell G. Gallagher

Tom Paine was a controversial figure in his time. He is still the subject of bitter debate. No matter what position one may take towards him, there is sure to be both agreement and disagreement with the expressed views.

He is an essential part of the history of the United States. To refuse to discuss him merely because he is a polemical figure would be both cowardly and deceptive. There is a whole school of thought today which would try to rule out debate in American schools and colleges. Strangely enough, those who oppose the teaching of controversial material are usually the same persons who insist that we must also teach American history. They want us to teach history; but they don't want us to discuss conflicts of ideas. Their request is an impossible one. The plain fact is that history is shot through with differences of opinion. Either you do not teach history at all, or else what you teach includes past controversies.

There is, of course, one way to avoid the difficulty. You can do it the way it is done under totalitarian direction. Simply re-write it all. Lay down the line, select your facts, and twist and contort them until you build a picture to your liking. Then call that history and teach it. You certainly can do away with contention if you want to go in for lies and thought control. But if you want to deal with the truth, then you must accept the facts of history as it has been lived — filled with struggles among men and ideas and events.

Tom Paine was a rebellious and contentious man. He entered the American scene as a revolutionist, a pamphleteer whose writings fanned the flames of revolt against the British.

"These are the times that try men's souls." At the moment when Paine penned these lines on a drumhead by the campfire, he was with Washington's army in full retreat across New Jersey. Citizens and soldiers alike despaired of the Revolution as a lost cause; the British appeared invincible. To that moment of despair, Paine spoke.

"The summer soldier and the sunshine patriot," he said, "will, in this crisis, shrink from the service of their country; but he that stands it *now* deserves the love and thanks of man and woman. Tyranny, like hell, is not easily conquered; yet we have this consolation with us, that the harder the conflict, the more glorious the triumph."

His pamphlet was read to every corporal's guard of the dispirited Continentals on Christmas Eve, 1776. That very night, battling the ice floes and the blizzard, they crossed the Delaware and fell upon the sleeping Hessians. With the inspiring words of Paine to spur them, they won against tremendous odds the sorely needed victory.

In the seven weary years of struggle which followed, it was Tom Paine who wrote the necessary word for meeting each succeeding trial. Sixteen times he went to press with new pamphlets — parts of *The American Crisis*, as he called it. The first pamphlet began with the words, "These are the times that try men's souls." In the last of the series he wrote, "The times that tried men's souls are over."

What happened between these two writings is history — a history which Paine helped to make, a history which is crowded with conflict because it is the history of a desperate episode in man's long, continuing struggle to be free. As Paine put it, "America need never be ashamed to tell her birth." Conceived in revolution, this nation would be untrue to its heritage if ever its sons forgot the controversies which struck the chains and made us a free nation of free men.

It was Tom Paine who proposed to the thirteen colonies scat-

tered along the vast Atlantic coast line that they should call themselves by the grandiloquent name, " The United States of
America." It was Paine who exposed the Tories and excoriated
the slaveholders. It was Paine who challenged the might of wealth
and the power of pride in the name of freedom and of equality.
Paine's words inflamed a people, transforming a beaten and be-
draggled rabble in rags into the sword of righteousness.

He was born an Englishman. His father was a Quaker, his
mother an Anglican who became a Quaker. His later life saw
him attacking his fellow Quakers in Pennsylvania for their failure
to support the war. He also rejected the personal God of his
childhood faith and became a deist. Yet, throughout his life, he
never lost the sharpness of the ethical insight his early religious
training had given him; his Quaker conscience remained acute.

The goodly part of Paine's legacy to us is in his words, not his
deeds. Like many other men whose labors with the pen have been
influential, Paine was singularly unfortunate in his actions. He
seems to have had a predilection for doing the awkward thing
when it was least needed; and, aside from his writings, nearly everything he put his hand to came to naught. He was an inventor
who dreamed of building an iron bridge across the Schuylkill;
but the bridge was never constructed. He was a collector of taxes
who was put forward by his fellow government employees as
their champion in behalf of decent wages — for which he lost his
job. He sat in the National Convention of the newborn French
Republic and helped to frame the constitution of 1793 for that nation; but in the French Chamber his tongue failed him, for he
could not speak the language. He was not a man of glorious
deeds, however brave his words. Aside from his written contribution to the American Revolution, most of his words were destined to get him into trouble.

In 1787 he returned to England. The French Revolution was
under way, and was bitterly attacked by Edmund Burke. Paine
promptly issued a counterblast to Burke, calling it *The Rights of*

Man. His attack was so vigorous that he was forced to flee for his safety from London. If the police courier had not arrived twenty minutes after the cross-channel boat had sailed for Calais, Paine would have languished in a British prison instead of sharing in the debates of the new government of France. Finding himself out of sympathy with the excesses of the French Terror, he opposed the Jacobins and was thrown into prison. He would have lost his head under the knife of the guillotine if Robespierre had remained in power long enough to see the order executed.

Eventually returning to the United States, Paine lived out the last years of his life in poverty and ostracism, an unkempt and slovenly figure, enjoying almost universal contempt or neglect. He was denied the right to vote when he presented himself at the polls in New Rochelle in 1802 — a crushing blow to one who had so vigorously championed the political rights of all men. And when he was buried in 1809, his seventy-two years of battling for human freedom were remembered by only five persons who cared or dared to attend the funeral — a French woman and her son, a Quaker, and two Negroes.

Efforts have been made by certain writers of fiction to twist the plain facts of Paine's life into an epic of proletarian tragedy. From the typewriter of one pro-communist author, Paine emerges as a combination of the angel Gabriel and Comrade Lenin. The transparent motive of such writing is to try to claim Tom Paine for the Soviet cause. This act of literary vandalism is on a par with the naming of the principal pro-communist educational center in New York City for Thomas Jefferson. We can readily admit that Tom Paine was a controversial figure; but we need not admit that everyone who pursues a cause to his own hurt is a communist. Tom Paine is a controversial figure; but he fought for human rights and the dignity of man, not for state tyranny and the forced labor camp. Let's rescue Paine from those who wear his mask to hide their own treachery.

Another accusation from which Paine must be rescued is the

assertion that he was an atheist. Paine was no atheist. Like Washington, Jefferson, and Lincoln, he was a deist. His thoughts on religion are set down in *The Age of Reason*, a work composed during his sojourn in France, when his disappointment with the terroristic excesses of the French Revolution led him to turn from politics to religion. Much of this work was composed in the Luxembourg prison, without benefit of a library. It is a remarkable exhibition of what a mature man's insight can do with his memories of childhood religious instruction. It is a profoundly religious book; but it is an ignorant book, written without comprehension of what a mature theistic faith professes.

To understand *The Age of Reason*, we must put ourselves back into the thought of the early nineteenth century. The work of Descartes and Bacon was coming to full fruition in religious and scientific thought. This thought rejected the idea of a personal God and accepted instead the idea of a God who had created the universe and then gone off and left it. Paine accepted this and believed that the whole of his creation exhibited the nature and character of the deity, but the deity himself no longer interfered with what he had created. This deistic view was quite prevalent among men of Paine's day for at least two very good reasons. First, science had already demonstrated that the view of the world formerly held by most religious people was no longer tenable; and, second, religion and theology had not yet devised the tools of modern scholarship and biblical criticism which have since reduced most of Paine's indictments of orthodoxy to commonplaces of general acceptance.

A special circumstance further explains the vehemence of Paine's own rejection of what he thought to be the faith of theists. He was not an educated man. He was innocent of any but the most meager formal schooling, due to the fact that from earliest youth he had to work for a living. And while he was an omnivorous reader, he tended to read not with his mind but with his prejudices, as many others, both educated and uneducated, have done. His lifetime of study of religious matters thus resulted in his elaborating a devastating argument against a theistic faith and a biblical religion; but what he was destroying was mostly a straw man dressed up in the clothes of boyhood recollections. There is nothing to indicate that Paine had any great familiarity with the writings of the distinguished men of faith of his own day, who were constructively bringing religious thought up to date in the newly emerging scientific world. Many subsequent readers of Tom Paine, particularly those who likewise are ignorant of what their contemporaries in theology and religion are actually saying and writing, are led to reject a theistic faith because they take at face value the empty abstractions which Paine attacks.

Paine had two motives in writing *The Age of Reason*. One was political, the other religious. We must bear in mind that he wrote in France while the Republic was being taken over by despotism. It must also be remembered that the reactionary role played by clerical forces in the French revolution had made that revolution essentially an anti-religious and anti-clerical effort. Tom Paine saw these things and regretted them. As one writer put it, Paine published *The Age of Reason* because he feared " that the growth of atheism threatened the existence of the only true religion, deism, and because he was determined to save republicanism from despotism." Far from being anti-religious, Paine was a man of profound reverence and humility who wanted to save religion as he knew it from being destroyed by anti-religious revolution as he saw it. At the same time he wanted to save the revolution from the destruction which it inevitably was to deserve because of its disregard for religious values. Far from being " a filthy little atheist," as Theodore Roosevelt called him, Paine poured his heated efforts into an attempt to save religion from atheism. He therefore stoutly supported deism and courageously attacked atheism.

Like Jefferson, Paine carried into his new-found deism all of the moral fervor and ethical insight of the theistic religion in which he had been raised. So profound and all-embracing was his moral conviction that he found it necessary almost to return to theism in order to support his ethic. He concludes Part One of *The Age of Reason* with these words: " The moral duty of man consists in imitating the moral goodness and beneficence of God, manifested in the creation toward all His creatures. Seeing, as we daily do, the goodness of God to all men, it is an example calling upon all men to practice the same toward each other; and, consequently, everything of persecution and revenge between man and man, and everything of cruelty to animals, is a violation of moral duty."

These words had just been written when the police battered on his door to take him away to prison as an enemy of the despotism established under Robespierre. Here was a man who *was* revolutionary! Living under revolutionary tyranny, he called for the ending of persecution and revenge. Living under blatant atheism, he called for a recognition of the moral goodness and beneficence of God. He believed so deeply in the moral responsibility which is essential to man's freedom that he spoke out against the immorality of despotism which, in the name of atheism and under the guise of revolution, was crushing the spirit of man with an all-pervading terror and fear. The moral basis of Paine's deism makes it almost theistic, and strongly against atheism. Those who try to pervert Paine's writings and life so as to make him sympathize with the contemporary practices of communism in its rejection of God, its violation of morality, and its espousal of atheism do not tell the truth about Tom Paine. They are just as much in error as those who try to paint him as the kind of revolutionary who would tolerate the massive, monolithic despotism of the Soviets.

As far as religion is concerned, Paine suffered from having to make his peace with Christianity in a day when the fruits of modern scholarship were not yet available, and when much of the Church (particularly in France) had identified itself with political reaction. The remarkable thing is not that he came out of this experience a deist rather than a theist, but that he came out of it a man of deep religious faith with an unblunted moral conscience. Writing from memory in his prison, he quoted in *The Age of Reason* the whole of Addison's paraphrase of the nineteenth Psalm which, set to Haydn's music, is a favorite in churches everywhere:

> The spacious firmament on high,
> With all the blue ethereal sky,
> And spangled heav'ns, a shining frame,
> Their great Original proclaim.

> In reason's ear they all rejoice,
> And utter forth a glorious voice;
> Forever singing as they shine,
> " The hand that made us is divine."

Those who disagree, as most of us do, with the particulars of Paine's religious conceptions will nevertheless do well to ponder Paine's words: " Let every man follow, as he has a right to do, the religion and the worship he prefers."

In reverting to the theme that the communists have no right to claim Tom Paine as a patron saint, it may be advisable to draw the threads of that argument together and state the reasons. They are four:

(1) One cannot reconcile Paine's tolerance with the intolerance which is the essence of communism. Here is what Paine wrote: " I do not mean by this declaration to condemn those who believe otherwise; they have the same right to their belief as I have to mine. But it is necessary to the happiness of man that he be mentally faithful to himself. Infidelity does not consist in believing, or in disbelieving; it consists in professing to believe what he does not believe." Paine could not be a communist — he was tolerant.

(2) One cannot reconcile Paine's opposition to the despotism which succeeded the French Revolution with support of the despotism which succeeded the Russian Revolution. The whole of *The Age of Reason*, for which Robespierre ordered Paine guillo-

tined, proves this point. Paine could not have supported the Soviets.

(3) One cannot reconcile communist disregard for civil rights with Paine's espousal of the French Declaration of the Rights of Man. The right to be presumed innocent until proved guilty; to be unmolested in the holding of opinions, so long as one does not disturb the established order; freedom of communication and of speech, accompanied by due responsibility in the exercise of these freedoms — here are fundamental rights written into the American Constitution and the French Declaration which are daily denied under the Soviets. Paine approved of them. He is on the side of democracy, not of despotism. The communists cannot claim him.

(4) Paine's opposition to atheism puts him clearly at variance — irreconcilable variance — with communism which, with Marx, holds religion to be an opiate of the people. His purpose in attacking biblical theism was to save deism from atheism.

Actually, the American Communist Party, in its attempts to embrace Tom Paine, has knowingly tried to give him the kiss of death. For those who champion the tyranny of dictatorship know well that the spirit of free men must be broken if tyranny is to triumph. And one good way to break men's spirit is to destroy their faith in their leaders. Hence, the goal is to assassinate the character of Tom Paine by embracing him.

In addition to *The Age of Reason*, which is his treatise in defense of a deistic religion, Paine's principal writings are *Common Sense*, *The American Crisis*, and *The Rights of Man*. The first of these was written in January 1776, and was one of the most effective factors leading up to the Declaration of Independence six months later. The second, written in sixteen brief pamphlets during the long years of the Revolutionary War, rallied flagging spirits and put new nerve and sinew into the disheartened Continentals. The third was his answer to Burke's attack on the French Revolution, written in the early days of that Revolution, before it had passed into the phase of despotic terror. There were, of course, numerous lesser writings which, published in a collection, make a volume nearly twice the size of his major works. Paine was a prolific and furious writer.

He was extraordinarily sure of himself. He was forever championing The Right — a kind of formal abstraction in his mind. He never tolerated the imperfect, and was always impatient with compromise. He was naturally rebellious by disposition, and also possessed an unusually sensitive conscience. With these characteristics, he was a happy fighter against the idea that any man was rightfully the master or superior of another. His life and work were dedicated to an unrelenting attack against privilege and power in any form.

If he has never occupied the position which might have been his in American history, the fate of the controversial character in the history of a country is the explanation. Who has ever honored the man who was temperamentally a rebel? Who has made a hero of the professional agitator? Only those who are themselves agitators by temperament and rebels by profession. But in our day, it is necessary for the professional agitators and rebels to pervert or hide the moral and religious components of Paine's character if they wish to espouse him in order to discredit him among lovers of freedom.

The wiser part for those citizens who share the great American heritage of belief in moral freedom, with its accompanying moral responsibilities, would be to accept with humility the arrogant assurances of Paine's legacy, to welcome the rebel back to our ranks and let him pipe again the "Spirit of '76." We can use a bit of it today.

This is true because the supreme danger within our own democracy comes not only from domestic and foreign communists but also from the demagogues who sow suspicion to reap power. Let us answer them with deeds to match Paine's matchless words.

"Suspicion and persecution are weeds of the same dunghill," he wrote. The demagogues who in our day of the American crisis sow suspicion to reap the fruits of power have long since seen that suspicion sown with a profligate hand quickly gives root also to persecution. They know that these twin evils will choke the sentiments of mutual confidence and make free men an easy prey.

These are the times that try men's spirits. The timid idealist and the fair-weather liberal will, in this crisis, fear to take a stand for human freedom and human rights; but he that stands *now* will find his faith renewed and his courage not wanting. Demagoguery, like all tyranny, wears a smiling and evil face; but the hour of decision has come. Who deserts the vanguard of freedom now, sinks to the rear with the slaves. But he who hurls the big lie back into the lying teeth and stands his ground will keep the faith. He will, in the spirit of Tom Paine, deserve the affection and gratitude of his children and his children's children.

2

Thomas Jefferson

William Bradley Otis

William Bradley Otis, professor emeritus of English at the College of the City of New York, was a government lecturer in France on "The Terms of the Treaty of Peace," 1919. He is the founder of the plan requiring a knowledge of the United States Constitution as a requisite for high-school graduation. He is also the author of *American Verse, 1625–1807: A History* and co-author of *An Outline History of English Literature* and *A Survey History of English Literature.*

Thomas Jefferson

William Bradley Otis

On the face of a mountain in South Dakota, Gutzon Borglum has sculptured four gigantic heads — the heads of George Washington, Thomas Jefferson, Abraham Lincoln, and Theodore Roosevelt. For countless generations to come this Rushmore Memorial will stand as reminder of the grandeur and glory of American democracy. Would it not have been appropriate had the sculptor given us, also, the head of James Madison, the "Father of the Constitution," or of Benjamin Franklin, the only signer of the four great documents of our early history, namely, the Declaration of Independence, the Treaty of Alliance with France, the Treaty of Peace with England, and the Constitution of the United States. But of Washington, Jefferson, and Lincoln, there can be no question. They stand supreme among the builders and preservers of the Republic. Politically, Washington may be said to represent the Right, Jefferson the Left, and Lincoln perhaps a little left of Center. It has been said that radicalism furnishes the hope of the world and that conservatism maintains the world's sanity. In his own day Jefferson was considered a radical. Today he is recognized as the patron saint of all that is good in American democracy.

Thomas Jefferson was born in Albemarle County, Virginia, on April 13, 1743. His father, Peter Jefferson, was a surveyor and a landowner who became rich in slaves and acres. The mother, Jane Randolph, came from a well-to-do family of social prominence in Virginia. When seventeen years of age, Thomas Jefferson entered William and Mary College where he remained for two years. For the next five years he studied law at Williamsburg. In 1767, at the age of 24, Jefferson was admitted to the

Bar. But, although he was successful as a lawyer, the profession was distasteful to him. His taste was philosophic rather than legalistic. He detested the jargon of the law. Jefferson was, at this time, one of the richest young men in Virginia and the most learned. He was proficient in Greek, Latin, French, and Gaelic. Of all the men who attained fame and distinction in the formation and early days of the Republic, Jefferson was undoubtedly the best educated and the most cultured. In the words of James Parton, " he was a gentleman of thirty-two who could calculate an eclipse, survey an estate, tie an artery, plan an edifice, try a cause, break a horse, dance a minuet and play the violin."

In the spring of 1764, while attending a session of the Virginia House of Burgesses, Jefferson was electrified by a speech delivered by his friend, Patrick Henry, with its historic climax: " Caesar had his Brutus, Charles the First his Cromwell, and George the Third may profit by their example! " It was at this time that Jefferson adopted as his motto: " Resistance to tyrants is obedience to God." Jefferson, himself, was no orator and rarely attempted public address. But among his contemporaries his reputation for clear thinking and lucidity of expression was widespread. When, therefore, it was decided that the time was ripe to issue a Declaration of Independence, the committee appointed for the purpose unanimously chose Jefferson to draft what has become an immortal document. In his autobiography Jefferson remarks: " The committee for drawing the Declaration of Independence desired me to do it. It was accordingly done." For seventeen days Jefferson worked on the draft, writing and rewriting, clarifying and polishing. Years later, in referring to this, he said: " Neither aiming at originality of principle or sentiment, nor yet copied from any particular or previous writing, it was intended to be an expression of the American mind."

And so it is. But it is also the voice of freedom-loving people the world over. To cavil at any part of the Declaration of Independence would seem a sacrilege. There is, however, one statement in it that from time to time has caused misunderstanding and controversy — the statement that "all men are created equal." What undoubtedly was meant by this assertion was only that all men are created equal in the sight of God and the law, and should have equal opportunity to develop their natural abilities and aptitudes. There are one-talent men, two-talent men and five-talent men. Jefferson himself was something of a scientist, architect, and inventor, and knew from study as well as from experience that the natural abilities of men are not equal. In a letter to John Adams dated October 28, 1813, Jefferson says: "The natural aristocracy I consider as the most precious gift of nature for the instruction, the trusts and the government of society, — may we not even say that that form of government is the best which provides the most effectively for a pure selection of those natural aristoi into the offices of government?" Men of mediocre mentality and limited natural ability have, with arrogance, too often misinterpreted the words "all men are created equal." It is unfortunate that this broad affirmative was not qualified in the Declaration of Independence.

Jefferson, the founder of the University of Virginia, believed that widespread popular education was an essential of a successful democracy. It was Jefferson who, in 1817, designed the free educational system now generally adopted in the United States. The elementary schools were to provide instruction in reading, writing, arithmetic, and geography. The high schools were to teach science and languages and to serve as preparation for the professions. However, because of his fear of coercion of any kind, Jefferson was opposed to compulsory education. Jefferson's plans for universal free education were violently opposed. Even thirty years later, when it was proposed to establish a Free Academy in New York City, the same kind of opposition appeared. An editorial in a New York newspaper of that time said: "The determination on the part of the pauper class among us to levy upon the active, industrious (and, if you please, affluent), portion of the community the expense of furnishing to the sons of the former a College Education through the Free Academy Project, must be viewed as one of the most shameless acts which disgrace these corrupt and degenerate times. It is a distinct and palpable assault upon the rights of property, with not as much of plausibility even as demagogues have usually been able to clothe their designs in." However, with the support of Horace Greeley and other liberals, the plan was finally submitted, in 1847, to a referendum of the people and was carried by a vote of five to one. The Free Academy, later to be called the College of the City of New York, was born. The spadework from which grew the City College of New York had been done by Thomas Jefferson in Virginia three decades earlier.

But Jefferson believed that the health and success of American democracy demanded, in addition to free education, the liberty inherent in free speech and a free press. He fought bitterly against the Alien and Sedition Acts of his time which were designed to curtail drastically both free speech and free press. More than any other American, Jefferson deserves credit for establishing throughout the land these two basic freedoms. Were he here today, Jefferson would no doubt be keeping a watchful and critical eye on Congressional inquisitions.

In a letter to Benjamin Rush (September 23, 1800) Jefferson said: " I have sworn upon the altar of God eternal hostility against any form of tyranny over the mind of man." There was yet another tyranny against which Jefferson girded himself for battle — the tyranny of religious bigotry and intolerance. The Established, or Anglican, Church was a state religion in Virginia. Methodists, Presbyterians, Quakers, and others were persecuted and often jailed for their open meetings and beliefs. Jefferson thought that men should have the right to worship God according to the dictates of their conscience. Like Franklin, Jefferson was a deist. He believed in God and tried to follow the moral code of

Jesus in the Sermon on the Mount. But he had little patience with creed and dogma. To Matthew Carey, in 1816, he wrote: " On the dogmas of religion as distinguished from moral principles, all mankind, from the beginning of the world to this day, have been quarreling, fighting, burning and destroying one another, for abstractions unintelligible to themselves and to all others, and absolutely beyond the comprehension of the human mind." And in a letter to Dr. Benjamin Waterhouse he said: " To love God with all thy heart and thy neighbor as thyself, is the sum of religion." After a long battle against powerful opposition, the Ordinance of Religious Freedom became law and the principle of separation of Church and State was established. Incorporated in the Bill of Rights are the words: " Congress shall make no law respecting an establishment of religion or prohibiting the exercise thereof." And again we bow in homage to Thomas Jefferson.

In 1801, twenty-five years after the Declaration of Independence, Thomas Jefferson was elected the third President of the United States. Four years later he was elected to a second term by an electoral vote of 162 out of 176. So great was his popularity that John Adams predicted that he would be elected to a third term. But Jefferson had no such intentions. He said: " I determined to withdraw at the end of my second term. The danger is that the indulgence and attachments of the people will keep a man in the chair after he becomes a dotard, that re-election through life shall become habitual, and election for life follow that. General Washington set the example of voluntary retirement after eight years. I shall follow it." During his administration the freedoms for which he had fought so courageously in earlier years were consolidated and made fundamental in the American way of life.

In 1803, at a price of $15,000,000, the " Louisiana Purchase " was negotiated with Napoleon. It was probably the greatest real estate deal in history. It added to the Republic practically all of the land lying between the Mississippi and the Rocky Mountains. Never since Manhattan Island was purchased from the Indians for $24.00, had there been such a profitable transaction.

Jefferson's admonition against "entangling alliances" followed Washington's advice in the Farewell Address. Washington had there intimated that we might later have commitments with other nations when we had attained greater political and economic strength. Even Senator Henry Cabot Lodge, Sr., prior to his quarrel with Woodrow Wilson, had stated in an address at Baltimore: "Nothing that Washington ever said or did would lead us to infer that, were he alive today, he would not be heartily in favor of a League of Nations." So, too, should Jefferson's warning against entangling alliances be thus interpreted at the present time.

In the political campaign of 1952, a prominent member of the Democratic Party stated that if Jefferson were alive today he would be an enthusiastic supporter of the New Deal. That he would still be a Democrat is certain. That he would also be in complete sympathy and accord with desires for more widespread, increased, economic well-being, is equally certain. All his life he had fought for the interest and the happiness of the common man in whom he had complete confidence. But it is certain, also, that he would have been critical of some things that characterized the latter days of the New Deal. For instance, he would have been appalled at the venality and corruption in high places. No breath of scandal touched his own administration of eight years. He did not believe in extravagance nor in the theory that government can spend its way into prosperity. His own official budgets were always balanced. "Alert and on guard" would have been his cry as he saw the long tentacles of government ownership and control, which he had fought in the days of Alexander Hamilton and the Federalists, reaching out further and further and sucking up exorbitant taxes to meet huge deficits. "That government is best," he said, "which governs least."

Jefferson, who advocated states rights and local autonomy,

would, I think, have protested the attempt of the New Deal to tax municipal and state bonds, a design fortunately declared unconstitutional by the United States Tax Court and affirmed by the United States Circuit Court of Appeals. The power to tax is still the power to destroy. Jefferson, however, had a flexible mind — a mind that could adapt itself to changed conditions. Indeed, he even advocated a complete revision of the Federal Constitution every twenty years. Had he lived through the last two decades of the New Deal he, too, would have recognized the necessity for stricter controls than were required at the beginning of the nineteenth century. He would have seen that the astounding so-called progress in this all too scientific age had greatly complicated our problems, that under modern conditions we are forced to accept more and more external controls in order to insure survival, that more and more green and red lights, stop-signals and other devices are necessary to control the complex congestion and confusion of modern life. While admitting all this, Jefferson would have insisted that the control must be *self*-control through free and unhampered education — democratic control by the people themselves rather than control by a powerful, self-perpetuating, political bureaucracy. It thus seems not unlikely that if Jefferson who, as we have said, favored a revision of the Constitution every twenty years, were alive today he might also be in favor of an occasional political change and readjustment.

During Jefferson's administration life in the White House was democratically simple. Balls, levees, and formal state dinners were abolished. Abolished, also, were the rigid rules of precedence and etiquette that had been observed by Washington and Adams. Never more than twelve persons were entertained at a time and they were seated at a round table, perhaps suggested by the fabled Round Table of King Arthur. The table was round so that in the seating no one should have precedence over another. As Jefferson said: "Nobody shall be above you, nor you above anybody."

Even in those early days the President found the duties of his office difficult and burdensome. He complained that he had no time for reading and philosophic meditation. Then, too, the expenses of office worried him. In his first year as President he spent over $32,000 on a salary of $25,000. At the end of his second term he was more than glad to retire. "Within a few days," he said, "I shall retire to my family, my books and farms, and having gained the harbor myself, shall look on my friends still buffeting the storm, with anxiety indeed, but not with envy. Never did a prisoner, released from his chains, feel such relief as I shall on shaking off the shackles of power."

The more we study the life of Jefferson, the more wonderful seem his accomplishments. On his epitaph, written by himself, we read: "Here was buried Thomas Jefferson, author of the Declaration of Independence, the Statute of Virginia for religious freedom, and father of the University of Virginia." To him more than to any other American do we owe the blessings of universal education and of freedom of speech, freedom of press, and freedom of religion. History has been said to be the lengthened shadow of great men. Men of Jefferson's stature are, indeed, rare. But a great crisis usually produces a great leader. The crisis of 1776 produced Washington and Jefferson; the crisis of 1861, Abraham Lincoln. Let us hope that in today's crisis, as great or greater than any that have preceded, a champion may arise to lead us with the vision, the wisdom, the courage, and the integrity of Thomas Jefferson.

Henry Neumann, sometime instructor of English at the College of the City of New York and lecturer on ethics at the University of California, is now Leader of the Brooklyn Society for Ethical Culture. He is the author of *Education for Moral Growth; Modern Youth and Marriage; Lives in the Making;* and *Spokesmen for Ethical Religion.*

3

Horace Mann

Henry Neumann

Horace Mann

Henry Neumann

American cities have their statues to soldiers and sailors, but how many statues are there to Horace Mann? Many good citizens have scarcely even heard of this person to whom, more than to anyone else, we owe the fact that America has better public schools than were thought possible before Mann's time. A few public schools are named for him, but to the graduates of most such schools, he still is only a name.

Tax-supported schools for everybody are now so much a matter of course that we can scarcely imagine a time when there were none. But New York City's public schools are just a mere century old, for tax-supported schools, free for everybody, came into existence in that city only in 1853. Before that time, those who could afford it paid for the teaching of their children while the poor went without, or else attended the classes offered as a charity by the various churches. But even these church schools did not reach all the children of the poor. The year 1801 saw the first free school for poor white children whose parents were not enrolled in any sect provided by a Woman's Society who engaged a " widow woman of good education and morals as instructor " at $150 a year. A philanthropic group, the Public School Society, was organized in 1805 under the leadership of Mayor De Witt Clinton to raise funds for educating poor children exactly as private organizations provide homes for orphans or settlement houses. In 1818 the Public School Society was voted a subsidy by the state legislature. Only in 1853 did New York reach the point where the tax-supported schools for everybody which we know now, came into being. The same can be said of almost all the eastern states. Public opinion takes time to inform and arouse. The work was done by men like Horace Mann.

His home state, Massachusetts, was the pioneer colony to establish any public schools whatever. Children had to learn reading and writing before they entered — at the common age of eight. The schools were supported by public taxes, as was the church, for all citizens were members of the Congregational church. The religious town and the civil town were one. The first of those schools was established in Dorchester as early as 1639. This fact illustrates a superb thing in the tradition of that Puritanism at which many people find it so easy to sneer. Wherever Calvinism flourished, it was strong for educating the young, old, and those in between. This was true of Calvinism in France, Switzerland, Holland, Scotland, and New England. " Where the ground was too stony to raise grain, they planted schools to raise men."

But great movements have their periods of decline as well as of strength. A century ago New England's free schools were very inefficient compared with the private schools which the growing wealth of these industrial states made possible. But this increasing wealth and the fact that the citizens were no longer of the one religion helped to promote the movement for public schools. The use of steam power encouraged the building of factories. Towns sprang up, many of them growing three times as fast as the rest of the state. In 1820 there was no town of Lowell at all. Two decades later it had a population of 20,000. Horace Mann shrewdly used the argument that educated persons spend more money than an illiterate community. Economists of the day like Wheland pointed out how education excites people to exertion where ignorance encourages indolence. Thomas Cooper stressed the point that people who could read and write made more intelligent and more reliable employees. Besides, the workers were getting dangerous ideas, to quote Cooper's own words, " about equal division of property and the right of the poor to plunder the rich." The workers themselves were growing in power and were now demanding education as a right in contrast with education as a charity from the rich. All these influences helped to promote the movement for public schools where none existed or, as in Massachusetts, the movement for those *better* schools to which we are so greatly indebted to Horace Mann.

His leading motive was a simple, direct, moral passion — the fervent desire that America should measure up to the greatness of the promise implied in democracy. A century ago America was closer to the Revolutionary War and the War of 1812. It was still under the spell of the boasters, the flag-waving patriots who were satirized so deservedly by Charles Dickens in *Martin Chuzzlewit*. The worst aspect of this frantic boasting was that it left large areas of the country utterly contented with their ignorance. Mann understood the simple fact that the more contented a voter was, the greater the harm to America. There were many such people in that day. The story is told of how at the end of a political speech by someone who made a great show of big words, one listener jumped up and cried, " If you can spell all them words you used, you got my vote." Mann knew that getting rid of a king was a relatively easy task, but that the way to the true dignity of free men was long and arduous. Freedom was not at all bought and fully paid for in 1776 and 1812. It was his part to help that freedom acquire more mind and more conscience, as he wrote, " by watering the whole land with the streams of knowledge. It is not enough to have here and there a beautiful fountain playing in palace gardens. Let it come like the abundant fatness of the clouds upon the thirsting earth."

Horace Mann was born in 1796 in the town of Franklin, Massachusetts, a city which has the honor of being the first in America to have a public library. Benjamin Franklin was so pleased with the tribute the pioneers of the town paid him by giving it his name that he made it a gift of some hundred books. Mann's mother, a widow, was too poor to send her children to a private school. Indeed, she could not afford to buy the textbooks which in those days even in the public schools were bought by the parents themselves. The boy Horace paid for his books by braiding straw into long strips, to be sold to a hat factory. He used to say in public that he was astonished how men could understand so well the ways to make horses and cattle healthy and strong, while their own children were puny, distempered, and chronically ill. He wondered why there were ten professors of pugilism in the community to only one professor of physical education in the seminaries of learning. Indeed, what crowds would lay down money at the box office today just to see children improve their health?

Until Mann was fifteen, he never went to school more than ten weeks for an entire year. The studies were predominantly reading, writing, and arithmetic, a hard grind of slavery to the book, with learning chiefly a matter of cramming the memory, with no concern given to interest the children in the job nor much attention paid to individual differences. Thanks to people like Mann, that kind of barren schooling has more and more been discredited even though a few rugged souls like Mann himself somehow did learn under it, or perhaps in spite of it. What it did for the great mass of children was to fill them with a lifelong revulsion from books. So it did its part to encourage that lowbrow scorn for books under which America has long been handicapped. We still have a few lowbrows in every community, mistrusting any man in public office who ever reads a book, unless it is a western. Some are like the Nazis in 1933 burning books they cannot understand or just disliking them for views different from their own. They are backed by multitudes who simply ignore books and never buy one.

Mann succeeded in getting into Brown University, after which he went into the practice of law, and then into politics. Here, too, his life was a hard struggle. He had that New England conscience which is easier to ridicule than to imitate. He had endorsed notes for a brother; and when the brother failed, he took it upon himself to clear the good name of his family by paying off the debts. His wife records that there was a time when on many days he was unable to buy a dinner. He rose rapidly in politics. When he was thirty-one, he was elected to the Massachusetts House of Representatives. There his first speech was to ask for repeal of the law which taxed everybody to support the Congregational church. Nine years later he was elected president of the Massachusetts State Senate. The law establishing the first State Hospital for the Insane was largely his work.

Had he chosen to stay in politics, his name might have been better known today. Instead, in 1837, to the utter astonishment of people who did not know the kind of person he was, he consented to fill a position of quite minor importance. The Massachusetts legislature reorganized its State Board of Education; and Mann accepted appointment as secretary to this board. The year 1837 was the time of the worst financial depression which had yet afflicted our new country. As everybody had to economize, the towns cut down on their schooling. The teachers, who had never been any too well paid, were now paid still less. The office of Secretary of the State Board of Education carried a salary of $1,500 a year with no provision for traveling or any other kind of expense. Any lawyer who had already risen as high in politics as Mann would have been looking ahead at that time to a much more handsome income. But here again we see in Mann the splendid side of the Puritan character.

It is not true that all Americans care chiefly for money. Even those who do make money may want to be of use in the world and take a pride in offering a commodity or a service which people need. Some care so much to be of use that they are satisfied if they can earn even the barest living. Mann was like that. As an American who loved his country, he had the profoundest faith in democracy. He saw clearly how much there was in our national life which was a disgrace. There was, even in those days, much corruption in our politics. Elections were often stolen in ways that the most crooked machine today cannot surpass. Mann saw that huge numbers of voters were ignorant. But, like Lincoln, he was convinced that the plain people of America wanted by and large to do the right thing and that the way to get them to do so was to begin in childhood with schools for everybody. That is why, with religious consecration, he dedicated to this enterprise the talents which might have brought him eminence in politics.

His task was far from easy. There were persons who opposed tax support for the schooling of other people's children. Mann was a Unitarian; and to the orthodox majority this was equivalent to being an atheist. Bigotry (which Carl Sandburg called the attitude of the fish who, preferring to swim, cannot see why birds choose to fly) still afflicts us. About thirty years ago a Brooklyn priest opposed the idea of bringing the College of the City of New York into his borough because, he said, it would simply " miseducate another lot of atheists and bolsheviks." A century ago the same enlightened spirit showed itself in another unenlightened direction. There were taxpayers who objected to establishing the Free Academy, as the College of the City of New York was first called. " Why," they asked, " should we be taxed to educate the sons of Irish immigrants? "

Opposition on many grounds delayed but did not defeat the movement to which Mann gave his strength. In some states the schools had to be made entirely free, maintained by taxes, cleansed of the taint that they were only for paupers. In Massachusetts they had to be better supported so that the schooling they offered could be improved. Mann's job was to do this. He did it by going about the state investigating conditions and arousing public sentiment. At that time he published twelve now historic Annual Reports.

In the first report he showed up the utter wretchedness of most of the physical equipment. Muscles and bones were tortured six hours a day on benches without backs, which were too high or too low from the ground. No wonder mischief was done for sheer relief! The buildings were often miserable shacks, with all the classes in one room. Many a farmer would have scorned to use these as a barn — like the one with the hole in the roof that let in the rain while another hole in the floor carried the rain out.

With few exceptions, children hated school. To keep them at their work, teachers employed that easy instrument of the incompetent, the switch. Horace Mann saw early that corporal punishment was bad for the children in appealing to so debasing an emotion as fear. It turned what should be free labor into slave labor: " You cannot open blossoms with a storm but under the genial influences of the sun." " The very blows which beat arithmetic and grammar in, beat confidence and manliness out." "They lead to hatred, fraud, lying, revenge." Such methods were bad for the teacher himself because they allowed him to be as inefficient as he chose. In spite of being bred in the Calvinist tradition that children were born depraved, Mann was convinced that children might be led to behave like human beings in the classroom and to study successfully, if they were genuinely interested, if the teachers took the trouble to teach so well that the children would genuinely want to learn of their own accord and would not think the teacher an enemy to be outwitted at every turn. Bad as many of our schools are today, America has certainly learned this much. But to get the communities to learn it during the twelve years when Mann was secretary was a terrific undertaking. He organized meetings. Few, if anybody, came to them. On one occasion not a single person was present except the janitor, while across the street a hall was packed to hear a windbag politician.

Mann was also interested in abolishing Negro slavery. A century ago, it may surprise some of us to be told, only the minority even in Massachusetts dared to call themselves abolitionists. Most of the respectable and powerful people wanted no change. This fact, too, led many to oppose Mann's ideas about schools. The teachers themselves in the public system resented his criticisms. Because he recommended the educational ideas of the Swiss Pestalozzi which were being used in the schools of Prussia, and which were better than most of the methods employed here, he was called un-American. Every occupation tends to breed in people a kind of dry rot which makes them regard innovators as traitors, cranks, and nuisances.

In consequence, Mann's efforts called for all his strength and a good deal more. In the diary which he kept we read: "I might almost be trying to batter down Gibraltar with my bare fists." But he was mastered by a faith which he set down in the diary in these words: "The time will come when education will be *reverenced* as the highest of earthly employments. That time I am never to see, except with the eye of faith; but I am to do something that others may see it, and realize it sooner than they otherwise would."

Results did appear. In 1839 Lexington, Massachusetts, had the honor of opening the first public training school for teachers in America. Today we should wonder how our public schools could get along without these agencies for preparing the teachers. A school of education is part of most of our country's colleges. If ever we grow discouraged at the slowness with which our public schooling improves itself, let us recall that the first public normal school in America did not appear until 1839. To help equip a residence hall for the future teachers, Mann sold his law library.

The twelve years of his labors for education brought fruit. Then in 1848 he went back into politics. Here, too, a great need summoned him. John Quincy Adams had died. That great Puritan, even though he had been President of the United States, had gone to Washington again, this time as a mere congressman, in order to fight for the abolition of slavery. When Adams died, Horace Mann was induced to succeed him in Congress. This he did in the interests of abolition, even though it meant opposing the famous senator from Massachusetts who preferred to soft-pedal on the anti-Slavery issue, Daniel Webster.

The fight in Congress had to be waged not simply for halting any further growth of the slave-power but for the basic right even to discuss the issues involved. Like other despots of that day or our own, leaders on the side of slaveholding wanted their opponents to be silent and succeeded in forcing through a series of " gag rules " for this purpose, in much the same way as their descendants employ the filibuster to defeat legislation against lynching or racial discrimination. Horace Mann's protest against this high-handed procedure deserves attention today:

I feel nonetheless inclined to discuss the question of freedom because an order has gone forth that it shall not be discussed. Discussion has been denounced as agitation, and then it has been dictatorially proclaimed that " agitation must be put down." Humble as I am, I submit to no such dictation, come from what quarter or what numbers it may. In this government, it is not tolerable for any man, however high, or for any body of men, however large, to prescribe what subjects may be agitated, and what may not be agitated. Such prescription is at best but a species of lynch law against free speech. It is as hateful as any other form of that execrable code, and I do but express the common sentiment of all generous minds, when I say that for one, I am all the more disposed to use my privilege of speech, when imperious men, and the sychophants of imperious men, attempt to ban or constrain me. . . . I hold treason against this government to be an enormous crime; but great as it is, I hold treason against free speech to be incomparably greater.

In 1852 the abolitionist group, then becoming a new political party known as the Free-Soil Party, nominated Mann for governor of his state. On the same day he was asked to preside over a newly established college at Yellow Springs, Ohio. This was Antioch College, which in our own day took on a new life when the distinguished engineer Arthur Morgan became its president. Mann accepted the Antioch position and remained there for seven

years until his death in 1859. His salary had been originally set
at $3,000 a year. Then it was reduced to $2,000, then to $1,500;
and even this was never paid in full. But he believed in his job
and stuck to it.

The character of the man is interesting. He had some of the
shortcomings that go with the Puritan training, making much of
matters, like smoking, which to us are trifles. He urged Richard H. Dana to rewrite *Two Years Before the Mast* so that it
could be used in the schools as a textbook which would convey
" some direct moral lesson."

But he was a man of forceful character, with a rugged honesty
which never failed him. As a lawyer he refused to defend clients
he knew to be guilty:

I well know . . . what the old lawyers say about its being right to
defend a known wrong side. I deny it all, and despise it. If a bad
man wants such work done, he shall not have my soul to do it with.
I should not like to catch the smallpox; but that would be a tolerable
disease, rather than to let a scoundrel inoculate me with his villainy.
Because he has committed violation Number One, shall I commit
violation Number Two in order to secure impunity to him by means
of what is called a Court of Justice?

His words recall how Abraham Lincoln took the same stand on
the ethics of the lawyer.

As we look ahead we see many points where the good work so
nobly advanced by this great American needs to be carried further. The fight for literacy has in the main been won. With relatively few exceptions, we no longer need to see that every child
in America learns to read and to write. For today and tomorrow
we are much more concerned over how people are to employ this
gift: we have seen that along with many splendid uses of such
knowledge, have come others which are a disgrace. It is not only
the illiterate who exhibit stupidities, vulgarities, brutalities, and
moral callousness. We might mention newspapers which, far
from promoting democracy, disgrace and block it.

We are forced today to think out more thoroughly what equality means. Mann insisted that the children who went to the little public school house should have an equal chance with the children in the private academy. Today there are many more communities that do offer such equal opportunity to learn to read and write. But even if every child in the country got the excellent schooling now offered in certain cities, we have still to learn in too many places that equality does not mean sameness. " Thingminded " children do not take to books as readily as those who are " word-minded." Those whose minds move at a quicker pace are obliged to waste time while slower minds are catching up. Artistic natures do not yet get everywhere the special opportunities offered to their kind in our best schools. Many rural schools are still far behind those in cities. Psychological service to prevent troubled spirits from seeking an outlet in delinquency is by no means as common as it should be. Children differ in their abilities. They are equal, however, in being entitled to the same chance for each to rise to his own highest level.

Another need is one which is forced on our attention by the intolerances fought by other great American liberals. If the Horace Mann who struggled for better treatment of the insane, for greater justice to debtors, for the abolition of slavery, for the right to debate all public issues freely were living now, he would be urging us to stand by our teachers, support and encourage those among them who are aware how the new age always brings new needs and who want to bring the teaching of today in line with these important demands. The chief danger to teachers today comes from those who want to make our schools thoroughly partial to the traditional (as they see it), and hostile to the needed new. Douglas Jerrold spoke of people who, out of respect for the old moon, won't even look at the new moon. Such persons think that Americanism means gazing at their own preferred part of the past. They forget that the heritage of liberty can be preserved only by waking up to the new claims which any genuine

freedom must honor. Free discussion is no luxury but a vital necessity. It is a menace only to the things that cannot stand the
light of investigation.

Many good causes summon us today. The spirit in which to
meet them is indicated in these words spoken by Horace Mann to
the students of Antioch College in the last commencement address
he delivered:

While, to a certain extent, you are to live for yourselves in this life,
to a greater extent you are to live for others. Great boons, such as
can only be won by great labors, are to be secured; great evils are to
be vanquished. . . . The disabilities of poverty; the pains of disease,
the enervations and folly of fashionable life; the brutishness of appetites, and the demonisms of passion; the crowded vices of cities,
thicker than their inhabitants; the retinue of calamities that come
through ignorance; the physical and moral havoc of war; the woes of
intemperance; the wickedness of oppression, whether of the body or of
the soul; the Godlessness of bigotry, — these are the hosts against
which a war of extermination is to be waged, and you are to be the
warriors. Never shrink, never retreat, because of danger; go into the
strife with your epaulettes on.

At the terrible battle of Trafalgar, when Lord Nelson, on board the
" Victory," bore down upon the combined fleets of France and of
Spain . . . a musket ball lodged in his spine. He knew the blow to
be fatal; but as he lay writhing in mortal agony, . . . for four hours
the energy of his will sustained his vitality; and *he did not yield to
death until the fleets had yielded to him.*

So, in the infinitely nobler battle in which you are engaged against
error and wrong, if ever repulsed or stricken down, may you always
be solaced and cheered by the exulting cry of triumph over some
abuse in church or state, some vice or folly in society, some false
opinion or cruelty or guilt which you have overcome! And I be-
seech you to treasure up in your hearts these my parting words: *Be
ashamed to die until you have won some victory for humanity.*

4

Ralph Waldo Emerson

Gabriel Richard Mason

Gabriel Richard Mason, who retired after fifty-two years as a teacher in the New York City school system, was for the final twenty-five years of that period the principal of the Abraham Lincoln High School, Brooklyn. He has lectured on philosophy and education at Hunter, Brooklyn, and City Colleges, as well as the Brooklyn Institute of Arts and Sciences, and the New School for Social Research. He is the author of *Spinoza's Idea of God* and *A Study of the Pantheism of Spinoza*.

Ralph Waldo Emerson

Gabriel Richard Mason

Ralph Waldo Emerson has been acclaimed not only as a great American literary figure, but also as an outstanding liberalizing force of the nineteenth century. While Thoreau gloried in the simplicity of his life spent in the rustic haunts of nature, and Walt Whitman emphasized in his poetry the true meaning of democracy, Ralph Waldo Emerson, with faith in the divinity of all individuals, expounded the philosophy of self-reliance with such force and fervor as to leave his effective imprint on religion, education, politics, and the general life of our people.

Emerson was no systematic metaphysician. He had studied the world's outstanding philosophers from Plato to Schopenhauer, and had also dipped into the pantheistic doctrines of the East; but he never set himself the serious task of finding logical answers to the mysterious problems which for five thousand years had troubled the minds and hearts of men.

It is true that Kant and his followers had aroused Emerson's interest in Transcendentalism, which taught that man can attain knowledge that goes beyond experience with phenomena. He soon became a strong exponent of this doctrine, with a firm belief in a Higher Spirit, in immortality, and in free will; yet he cannot be considered a clear-cut advocate of Idealism, because of his deep interest in the pantheism of Spinoza as taught by Coleridge, Wordsworth, and Carlyle, and in the Brahmanism of India as it unfolded itself in the ancient Vedas.

Emerson never synthesized these two philosophies; but his thinking was always so stimulating, and expressed with such charming and literary elegance that the citizens of America and Europe listened to the Concord sage, and were deeply impressed with his profound views. Though he never followed a direct line in his earnest ascent to philosophic truth, he managed to reach the sunlit peaks of metaphysical reflection by leaping impulsively from crag to crag.

Ralph Waldo Emerson, born in Boston on May 25, 1803, was the son of a minister, William Emerson, whose ancestors for six generations back were New England clergymen. His father, reputed to be an orthodox preacher, was undoubtedly a liberal in his views, for with much satisfaction he had read the radical writings of Priestley, and self-indulgently had digested *The Age of Reason* of Tom Paine.

Though his parents lived in indigent circumstances, Ralph was educated in the Boston schools and at Harvard. For a few years, while he postponed his studies for the ministry, he unenthusiastically taught school. In his notebook he wrote: "Now, I am a hopeless Schoolmaster, toiling through this miserable employment even without the poor satisfaction of discharging it well."

Finally, when he was almost twenty-two, he was admitted to the Theological Seminary at Cambridge. His work suffered from poor health; but in spite of this handicap, he was graduated and soon called to the Second Church of Boston. Rev. Dr. Ezra Stile Gannett, speaking at the ordination, prophetically urged the members to respect the independence of the newly chosen leader, even if he proved somewhat too radical for them.

In his first sermon, the young minister declared that he planned to use a freedom befitting the greatness of the Gospel, and that he was more interested in teaching right living than religious dogma. He warned his listeners that the hoary traditions of religion were subject to reform. "I don't intend to be an ecclesiastical policeman," he said; and all wondered how far into the precincts of strange heresies he would wander.

Two years later, he began to lose faith in the institutionalized church, complaining that there was little love in religion as it was then practiced, and that both congregations and temples were loaded with sham. He feared that pride and ignorance ruled much of the current preaching, and that frequently religious practices were both cold and cheerless. Perhaps churches as institutions were needed; but he hated to find himself imprisoned in them. It led him to believe that " in order to be a good minister, it was necessary to leave the ministry "; for it seemed to him that the theological profession was antiquated when it demanded that we worship in the dead forms of our ancestors.

Concerned with all these thoughts, and repeating the world-shaking words of Luther, " Here stand I, I cannot do otherwise. So help me, God, Amen! " he soon handed in his letter of resignation. In it he boldly stated his definite opposition to formalism. His resignation, much to his relief, was accepted, and Emerson found satisfaction in the freedom he could now enjoy to seek and speak the truth.

After returning from a nine months' trip to Europe, where he had the good fortune to meet Wordsworth, Coleridge, and Carlyle, he preached occasionally, and then started on his career as a lecturer in various cities of the United States. He immediately found great success on the platform, and for the next half century continued this work as his life's profession.

After a few lectures on science, representative men, and other miscellaneous topics, in which he always glorified the individual, Emerson delivered two talks, the Phi Beta Kappa Oration, and the Divinity School Address, which made history.

On August 31, 1837, he spoke to 215 members of the Phi Beta Kappa Society of Harvard. His speech was received with mixed feelings of " confusion, consternation, surprise, and wonder." James Russell Lowell commented, " What crowded and breathless aisles, what windows clustering with eager heads, what enthusiasm of approval, what grim silence of foregone dissent." He called this classic address, " our Yankee version of a lecture by Abelard." Oliver Wendell Holmes characterized it as " our intellectual Declaration of Independence."

The times, Emerson thought, called for a change. " Our day of dependence, our long apprenticeship to the learning of other lands draws to a close." He demanded that the scholar, instead of remaining a pedant, should transform himself into the " Man Thinking," and become a person of broad culture, and a citizen of action who would leave his impress on the world he lives in. Such a scholar with a spirit of self-reliance, taking advantage of the secrets of Nature, and of the great books of all time, would lose his timidity, and his inclination to imitate, to surrender to authority, and to defer to European culture. " Meek young men," Emerson reminded his hearers, " grow up in libraries, believing it their duty to accept the views which Cicero, which Locke, which Bacon have given; forgetful that Cicero, Locke, and Bacon were only young men in libraries when they wrote those books." This was a clarion call for action, self-reliance, and initiative, especially for America, which now was beginning to make slow strides in its intellectual and cultural development.

The other address, perhaps even of greater importance than " The American Scholar," was the discourse delivered to the Divinity School at Cambridge, on July 15, 1838. With profound attention, the audience in the much crowded room listened to Emerson as he emphasized the Universal Spirit, the One Will, and the One Mind which was active everywhere, and which awakened in the individual the religious sentiment. This sentiment was the equivalent of the emotion which translated itself into the words of Jesus, " I am divine; through me God acts; through me God speaks." But for Emerson these profound declarations were true for all men! Each person could truthfully say, " I am divine; through me God acts; through me God speaks! " For eighteen hundred years, these words had been misunderstood and misinterpreted. Thus Christianity became a myth and developed into a formal, dead religion. " This we must reject," Emerson insisted. The needed breath of life can come only through the direct love of God, and the immediate adoration of the eternal verities. These must supersede the mediator, who has been created through distortion and exaggeration. Let us recognize the divine element in all men, as well as in Jesus, the son of the Nazarene carpenter, the Jewish rabbi of Palestine, the social reformer extraordinary, and the noblest of men.

Some like Theodore Parker praised the address for its liberal views and its courageous demand for reform of the evils in the existing theology, yet most preachers were shocked, hurt, and disturbed by what they said was neither good divinity nor good sense. They called his talk a curious mixture of the German Kant, the French Cousin, and a pinch of Hindooism. It was, they said, full of illogical reasoning, inconclusive evidence, and unassimilated philosophy.

But Emerson stood firm and unmoved. He refused to enter into arguments with those who differed with him; but he never wavered in his individualistic views about Jesus the man, nor in his intuitive approach to religious truth. He took all criticism in his stride, saying: " Taunts and cries of hatred and anger, the very epithets you bestow on me, are so familiar in my reading, that they sound to me ridiculously old and stale." In a mood of defiance he added, " whilst I see that you must have been shocked, and must cry out at what I have said, I see too that we cannot easily be reconciled, for I have a great deal more to say that will shake you out of all patience." Many forward-looking men, though they did not agree fully with everything Emerson had said, admired " his free spirit and his free utterance," and prophesied the address would have a lasting effect on the religious thinking of our people.

Emerson's fame as a liberal reformer rests not only on the Phi Beta Kappa Oration with its tremendous influence on education and culture in America, and on the Divinity School Address with its emphatic break with religious formalism and tradition, but also on his expressed views in the field of politics.

Emerson cared little for political debates, but was always interested in political thinking about the woes and cares of practical life. He worshiped democracy, which to him was an outgrowth of self-knowledge, self-reverence, and self-reliance. He realized there were abuses in democracy, as well as latent virtues, and was optimistic enough to hope for the improvement of society, and for the efflorescence of our democratic institutions. He insisted that the main function of government is the development of self-reliant personalities. With each American living his own life to full capacity, the State would grow and prosper as the chief beneficiary of contributions made by all of these self-trusting, social-visioned citizens.

Naturally, with such views about the unique worth of personality, Emerson admired the valiant efforts of those who waged the anti-slavery campaign. When Congress rushed through the Fugitive Slave Law, he lost respect for our governmental authority for having passed what he called such " a filthy enactment." Emerson realized that we could neither have peace, nor a real Union of States, while slavery prevailed, and he shouted, " I will not obey, by God. Root out slavery; burn it up; pay for the damage; and let us have done with it." With former President John Quincy Adams, he advocated that our government purchase the slaves from the present owners, as England had successfully done in the West Indies. When it was estimated that this would cost two billion dollars, Emerson was confident that the sum would be paid for enthusiastically, " to dig away this accursed mountain of sorrow once and forever out of the world."

He not only entered the lists for the Negro slaves, but he also joined the women leaders fighting for their franchise. Though he cherished the chivalrous and romantic ideals of womanhood, and feared their disappearance, yet as a worshiper of the individual, he felt bound to fight in behalf of feminine freedom and sex equality.

On Tuesday, November 6, 1860, Emerson voted for Lincoln,

and was pleased with the results, characterizing as "sublime" the pronouncement of the masses of Americans against slavery. When the Civil War started, he called for sacrifices. "In a righteous cause," he said, "gunpowder smells good," and wrote the well-known lines,

> So nigh is grandeur to our dust,
> So near is God to man,
> When Duty whispers low, "Thou must,"
> The youth replies, "I can."

After meeting Lincoln, whom he described as a frank, sincere, well-meaning man with a lawyer's habit of mind, he enthusiastically supported him in the election of 1864. Rejoicing on his victory, Emerson remarked, "Seldom in history was so much staked on a popular vote. A nation is no casual combination to be dissolved lightly, or by stealth, or by violence." The day when Lee surrendered to Grant was a happy one. "Mankind," Emerson told his friends, "appeared in its best attitude around Mr. Lincoln in these recent experiences, and will aid him to use sanely the immense power with which the hour clothes him."

At the funeral services for the martyred president, held a few days later at Concord, Emerson spoke of his virtues and his inspired leadership in a great crisis. "His brief speech at Gettysburg," Emerson said, "will not easily be surpassed"; and he added, "His election to the Presidency was a triumph of good sense of mankind and of public conscience. Rarely was man so fitted to the event." As Emerson regarded the great ordeal through which Lincoln had passed, he rejoiced that principle, not expediency, had always been followed, that the Union had been saved, and that slavery had been destroyed forever with the newly-won rights for Negroes.

In addition to Emerson's liberal views on slavery, woman suffrage, the Civil War, and Lincoln, we find a wealth of profound thoughts in his essay on " Politics." These have a surprising ring of modernity. Fascists and Communists should note that according to the Concord sage, " the State is not superior to the citizen." He regards law as man's expedient to meet a particular case; therefore he says, " Laws are all alterable. Young civilians believe that any measure may be imposed on a people, if only you can get sufficient voices to make it a law. But the wise know that foolish legislation is a rope of sand which perishes in the twisting." Consequently, " the strongest usurper is quickly got rid of, and only they who build on Ideas build for eternity."

People sometimes wonder why we now have misgovernment. Emerson explains that " the form of government which prevails is the expression of what cultivation exists in the population which permits it."

His views on property have influenced legal and juridical thinking of today. He says, " Politics considers persons and property as the two objects for whose protection government exists. Of persons, all have equal rights in virtue of being identical in nature; but their rights in property are unequal," and adds, " The readily admitted principle that property should make law for property, and persons for persons, no longer looks so self-evident. Too much weight has been allowed in the laws to property." Statesmen today should bear in mind Emerson's injunction, " The only interest for the consideration of the States is persons; for the highest end of government is the culture of men."

With his usual insight, Emerson discusses democracy and radicalism. He prefers democracy to all other forms of government. However, he is aware of certain weaknesses in our politics. " Ordinarily," he warns us, " our parties are parties of circumstance, and not of principle. The vice of our leading parties is that they do not plant themselves on the deep and necessary grounds to which they are respectfully entitled, but lash themselves to fury in carrying out some local or momentary measure, nowise useful to the commonwealth."

" The spirit of our American radicalism " — this seems as true today as a century ago when Emerson said it — " is destructive and aimless. It is not loving; it has no ulterior and divine ends, but is destructive only out of hatred and selfishness."

He agreed with Jefferson in saying that the less government we have the better; and with staunch optimism looked forward to democratic progress: " We think our civilization near its meridian, but we are yet only at the cock-crowing and the morning star." The great advance, he thought, would come through the introduction of love in government. " The power of love, as the basis of a State, has never been tried. Thousands of human beings might exercise towards each other the grandest and simplest sentiments, as well as a knot of friends or a pair of lovers."

With what prophetic aptness did Emerson dissect the evils of the political scene as they exist in the world today. Writing in 1847, he has the surprising answer for those who ask why Uncle Sam, in spite of the Marshall Plan, is hated in Europe today: " We do not quite forgive a giver. The hand that feeds us is in some danger of being bitten." " It is a great happiness to get off without injury and heart-burning from one who has had the ill-luck to be served by you. It is a very onerous business, this of being served, and the debtor naturally wishes to give you a slap."

Scores of other essays of Emerson affected life in America; but of these let us speak only of " Self-Reliance," an apotheosis of the individual, a hymn of praise for courage, heroism, and initiative. The thoughts therein expressed have served as moral dynamite to many generations of young Americans. Youth has been stirred by Emerson's words calling for originality and initiative: " To believe what is true for you in your private heart, is true for all of us, — that is genius."

Perhaps the most quoted line of Emerson is, " Trust thyself: every heart vibrates to that iron string." He goes on to explain, " These are the voices which we hear in solitude, but they grow faint and inaudible as we enter into the world, for society is everywhere in conspiracy against the manhood of every one of its members."

In this essay, Emerson boldly attacks conformity: "I am ashamed to think how easily we capitulate to badges and names, to large societies and dead institutions." And then Emerson makes the thought-provoking observation, "It is easy in the world to live after the world's opinion; it is easy in solitude to live after our own; but the great man is he who in the midst of the crowd keeps with perfect sweetness the independence of solitude." Why does Emerson object to our conforming to usages that have been dead? Because it scatters our force, it loses our time, and it blurs our character; but at the same time he reminds us: "For non-conforming the world whips you with its displeasure."

He also inveighs repeatedly against consistency: "With consistency a great soul has simply nothing to do. Speak what you think now in hard words, and tomorrow speak what tomorrow thinks in hard words again, though it contradict everything you said today."

Never has anyone spoken so inspiringly as Emerson did on the old theme, "Be a man." "Let a man know his worth, and keep things under his feet. Let him not peep, or steal, or skulk up and down, with the air of a charity boy, a bastard, or an interloper in the world which exists for him." For this reason, Emerson refuses to worship the past: "Man is timid and apologetic. He is no longer upright; he does not say, 'I think,' but quotes some saint or sage."

He challenges us with our duty to speak the truth: "We have become timorous, desponding whimperers. We are afraid of truth, afraid of freedom, afraid of death, and afraid of each other."

In this spirit of self-reliance, Emerson also sharply criticizes people who mumble selfish prayers: "Prayer as a means to effect a private end is meanness and theft. As soon as the man is at one with God, he will not beg. He will then see prayer in all action,

like the prayer of the farmer kneeling in his field to weed it."
He therefore urges us all to be independent, and stand squarely
on our own feet. " It is only as a man puts off all foreign support
and stands alone that I see him to be strong and to prevail. Nothing can bring you peace but yourself."

It is difficult to estimate the amount of courageous, pioneering,
upstanding Americanism that seeped into several generations of
our citizens from Emerson, who wrote these heart-stirring, un-
traditional, iconoclastic words about initiative, conformity, consistency, truth-telling, prayer, and independence. The same may
be said of the wisdom and the inspiration to be found in many of
his other essays like " Compensation," " Heroism," " Love," " History," " Friendship," " Nature," and " Spiritual Laws " which for
a century have silently and subconsciously shaped the thoughts
and actions of our American people of yesterday and of today.
His wise counsel, his words of inspiration, and his emphatic and
important reforms in education, religion, politics, and life in general have made Emerson the great American liberal of the nineteenth century, whose influence is being felt in a great measure
even at the present time.

5

Abraham Lincoln

Oscar Zeichner

Oscar Zeichner, associate professor of history at the College of the City of New York, is also administrator of the Social Studies program of the College. He has been a lecturer at Teachers' College, Columbia University, and he is the author of *Connecticut's Years of Controversy*.

Abraham Lincoln

Oscar Zeichner

It was only natural for the self-searching liberal of a few decades ago to suffer from uncertainty and confusion. New intellectual currents swept away many of his basic assumptions about the nature of man and society. The new tyrannies of our time, communism and fascism, challenged his belief in the inevitability of human progress, rejected most of the values for which he has striven, and imposed their rule upon hundreds of millions on all the continents of the world. Disillusioned and dismayed by the turn of events in history, it is not surprising that the liberal was often confused about the present and uncertain about the future.

An added factor to this confusion was the change in the meaning of liberalism itself. Eric Goldman tells us in his excellent survey of modern American reform movements that it is easy to silence any group by simply asking the question, " What is liberalism? " The philosophy of liberalism as it was understood in the nineteenth century has undergone tremendous changes. Those who supported Jefferson in 1800 would not easily recognize some of today's varieties of self-proclaimed Jeffersonians. And Lincoln, too, probably would have difficulty in reconciling his own principles with the views of some who now claim to speak in his name.

There may be confusion about the nature of liberalism, both past and present, and about some of the persons associated with liberal ideals in American history, but there are no awkward silences about Lincoln. More books are written about him than about any other American. He is undoubtedly our greatest political figure. Indeed, to most of us Lincoln has become the embodiment of American political aspiration and genius.

But we do not all agree on every detail of the Lincoln story. Lincoln scholars, for example, have reminded us of the complexity of his personality and beliefs in contrast to the traditional portrait which drew him in simple and obvious lines. Lincoln was actually a combination of different, and even of opposite traits, and among these were qualities both conservative and liberal. The idea that the " Great Emancipator " was conservative in any respect may upset the liberal skeptic, but it is not difficult to see Lincoln's respect for tradition. He certainly was no radical agitator; he was never known to urge hurried or unreasonable change. He was cautious and prudent, and he always preferred moderation to the extreme. Fundamentally, one can say that he generally wanted to preserve the best of the past even when he was espousing the cause of reform.

But Lincoln was no standpatter. On the contrary, the other, and the more basic part of his personal and political make-up was fundamentally liberal, humane, reformist. His best biographer has described him as " a tough minded liberal realist," a conservative in method, a liberal in principle, an advocate of peaceful evolutionary change in accordance with American traditions and ideals.

Lincoln's liberal outlook was undoubtedly shaped by his early experiences in the simple, rough, and even harsh frontier conditions that prevailed in the fast-growing communities of the Midwest. Here he saw democracy practiced on the level of everyday life. Here Lincoln learned to be strong and independent, and also to appreciate the values of warm friendship and sympathetic, unselfish consideration of his neighbors. While there is much of the myth in the traditional account which has Lincoln born into dire poverty, there is no doubt that economic and physical hardship was his lot as a boy and a young man; he himself always emphasized the fact that his early career was a chapter in " The Short and Simple Annals of the Poor." But he rose above the obstacles of frontier life, though he drew much that was good from its stern conditioning. He persevered, grew strong physically and morally; he became self-reliant and confident. But he never forgot his humble origins, and he never lost touch with the people from whom he came. In the words of Benjamin P. Thomas, " he grew beyond his old associates but not away from them."

This closeness to the people was a fundamental part of Lincoln's personal and political creed. He trusted his fellow citizens and drew inspiration and strength from them. He believed that when the people were properly informed they could govern themselves as no one man ever could. His democratic faith is caught in the aphorism attributed to Lincoln: " You can fool some of the people all the time, and all of the people some of the time, but you can't fool all the people all the time."

His faith in the common man was not only a matter of intellectual conviction; it was based on a deep understanding of the emotional needs of ordinary folk. When Lincoln became president he refused to shut himself off from the ordinary citizen who felt he had to see and talk to the leader of the nation. Defying threats to his life, Lincoln objected to the posting of special guards. He was no king, he said, and he wouldn't behave like one. It was important, he explained, that the people know that he would execute his responsibilities fearlessly. Very large numbers of callers pressed in upon him, but he refused at first to limit them. In justifying this enormous drain on his time and energy he once said of his visitors, " They do not want much and they get very little. . . . I know how I would feel in their place." Only the increasing and unremitting pressure of his presidential duties finally forced Lincoln to restrict his callers.

Lincoln's frontier background explains some facets of his liberalism. More significant were the principles by which Lincoln was to guide his political life — principles which mattered perceptibly as he grew in years and responsibilities.

Basic to his liberalism was a view of man and government that was derived from the philosophy of Thomas Jefferson and other eighteenth-century liberals. This philosophy is best known to

Americans in their most important political documents, the Declaration of Independence and the Constitution. Lincoln often found opportunity to describe his political creed. On one such occasion, as he was on his way to assume the awesome responsibility of the presidency of a nation facing the horrors of civil strife, he said: "I have never had a feeling politically that did not spring from the sentiments embodied in the Declaration of Independence. . . . I have often inquired of myself what great principle or idea it was that kept this Confederacy so long together." Was it merely the fact of separation from England, he asked? That could not be enough. The bond was something much more important, and it was to be found in the Declaration of Independence, which, in Lincoln's words, gave "liberty, not alone to the people of this country, but hope to the world for all future time. It was that which gave promise that in due time the weights should be lifted from the shoulders of all men, and that all should have an equal chance."

All the while that Lincoln was learning the practical tactics of the politician he never lost sight of this basic doctrine. He ultimately mastered the art of politics, and in so doing he found that he sometimes had to accept compromises. He saw that the essence of political achievement in a constitutional democracy was the gaining of what was possible. Sometimes an ideal objective might have to be temporarily subordinated, for he recognized that insistence on the impossible could only mean failure. Lincoln's statesmanship, as James Russell Lowell noted, was reflected in his "loyalty to great ends, even though forced to combine the small and opposing motives of selfish men to accomplish them." Lincoln never wavered in his loyalty to the great end of his political striving, the preservation and betterment of the democratic American republic.

In many ways and in different stages of his political career, Lincoln's words and deeds epitomized his democratic faith. His very first public announcement, delivered in the course of his campaign for the Illinois legislature, dealt with the importance of education. Fundamental to good citizenship, Lincoln emphasized, was knowledge and sound understanding. For without these, he asked, how could one appreciate the values of America's free institutions. One of the values of those institutions was the opportunity to move up the economic and social ladder. Abhorrent to Lincoln was the idea that any person should occupy a fixed status in life. He was fond of pointing to himself as an example of the self-made man, and he used that example to underscore his basic economic idea of advancement for all. He had also seen many other cases of dramatic success stories. In these instances America had duly rewarded hard work, initiative, perseverance, thrift, and enterprise. Lincoln believed that the doors to economic betterment must be kept open. Speaking in Hartford in 1860, he said, " I don't believe in a law to prevent a man from getting rich; it would do more harm than good. . . . When one starts poor, as most do in the race of life, free society is such that he knows that he can better his condition; he knows that there is no fixed condition of labor for his whole life."

American institutions could be endangered by an ignorant citizenry; they would certainly lose much of their democratic impulse if economic opportunity disappeared. But a free America in Lincoln's day, as well as in our own, faced dangers that came from other sources. Among these were mob violence and intolerance. Against these menaces Lincoln took an uncompromising stand. Not long after a radical abolitionist, Elijah Lovejoy, was murdered in Alton, Illinois, Lincoln denounced the viciousness of mob rule. Lincoln was no abolitionist; on the contrary, he disapproved of the extremist position the abolitionists took on the slavery question. But he could not support the proposition that the abolitionists should be checked by force. " There is no grievance," Lincoln said, " that is a fit object of redress by mob law."

Later in his career, as the growing dispute between North and South over slavery moved the nation closer to civil war, a new political movement, the Know-Nothing party, suddenly appeared, chiefly in the eastern states. Feeding on anti-foreign prejudices, and particularly on popular hostility towards Irish Catholics, the Know-Nothings rapidly became a powerful political force in the mid-fifties. Although many politicians made use of this new party to further their small ambitions, Lincoln would have nothing to do with it. What the Know-Nothing movement stood for ran counter to his own basic liberal tenets. How could he, Lincoln explained, who abhorred the oppression of Negroes, favor the degradation of white people. " As a nation we began," Lincoln said, " by declaring that ' all men are created equal.' We now practically read it ' all men are created equal except Negroes.' When the Know-Nothings get control," he continued, " it will read ' all men are created equal except Negroes and foreigners and Catholics.' When it comes to this," Lincoln said, he would prefer to emigrate " to some country where they make no pretense of loving liberty — to Russia for instance where despotism can be taken pure, and without the base alloy of hypocrisy." Fortunately for the nation the Know-Nothing movement died out as quickly as it was born.

A greater menace to our national existence than the Know-Nothing movement was the dispute over slavery which culminated in the Civil War. From the responsibilities that came to him as President during that terrible struggle, Lincoln could not flee. From his achievements during those war years came his greatness and also his martyrdom.

Bound up in this tragic conflict was the very complicated problem of Negro slavery. Early in the seventeenth century Negroes had been brought to the English colonies as unfree laborers. Slowly but surely slavery had taken root, particularly in the southern regions where a combination of economic conditions made it profitable to use increasing numbers of Negroes. Slavery, however, had also been established in all of the other colonies, and there was then no difference in the moral position on slavery between North and South. After the American Revolution slavery began to disappear in the northern states where it was less important as an economic institution, and where it was easier for the liberal ideals of the new American nation to bring about their reforming influences. It is interesting to note, however, that it was not until 1799 that New York provided for the freeing of the children of slaves; complete emancipation did not come in that state until 1827. New Jersey did not begin the job of doing away with slavery until 1804, and another forty-two years went by before slavery in that state finally came to an end.

In the South, however, special economic conditions and the social-psychological problems created by the large numbers of slaves made the task of realizing the philosophy of the Declaration of Independence, that "all men are created equal," much more difficult to attain. Actually, leading southern patriots had vigorously condemned slavery. Patrick Henry had denounced it as "an abominable" thing, a "system of violence and tyranny" in conflict with humanity, religion, and liberty. And Thomas Jefferson had doubted whether the new nation's freedom could be safe when some men deprived others of their God-given liberties. Unfortunately, this liberal sentiment was not strong enough to overcome the practical considerations demanding the continuation of slavery. The South's special institution was written into the Constitution and thus received its protection; and in the 1800's this labor system became even more important to the southern states when "King Cotton" took over that region's economy.

Lincoln's views on slavery developed slowly. There is the story that Lincoln took his position on the question as a result of a visit to a New Orleans slave market. Actually, for twenty years after that trip down the river Lincoln never referred to the incident, and the best Lincoln scholars question the influence of this experience in shaping his thinking. But there is no doubt that he was against slavery on principle, and he repeatedly said so. At the age of twenty-eight he defined the issues as he saw them: Slavery was unjust and was an evil influence on the nation. However, he made it abundantly clear that he opposed efforts to abolish it where it had a legal right to be. This remained Lincoln's position right to the outbreak of the Civil War. Such a liberal and moderate position was characteristic of Lincoln. On either side of it stood extremists. On the one hand were those who defended slavery as a positive good and who thereby denied the ideals which Lincoln equated with the American nation. On the other hand were those who in their zeal to rid the country of slavery were willing to defy the Constitution, and perhaps, to accept the dissolution of the republic.

Lincoln's principles were clear. Slavery was an evil, a " monstrous injustice." But under the Constitution it had the protection of the supreme law of the land, and, of course, as long as it was law it must be enforced. That is why Lincoln repeatedly reassured the South that he was opposed to any interference with slavery in that region. But when the issue of whether slavery could be extended anywhere in the territories under the jurisdiction of Congress developed in the mid-fifties, Lincoln took the unequivocal stand that Congress had the right to ban slavery in the territories and should do so. That was the argument that he developed in the famous debates with Senator Douglas.

It was our country's greatest tragedy that Lincoln's liberal and statesmanlike definition of this problem was unacceptable to extremists, particularly in the South. Emotions had been inflamed for decades, and by 1860 southern radicals, breathing fire and defiance, were prepared to shatter the Union.

As the incoming president in 1861, Lincoln was confronted with an awful responsibility. Civil war threatened to break out any day. Should he back down, retreat before the challenge of those who had already taken their states out of the Union? Lincoln did not shrink from the decision. The United States was a government of the people, and this form of government was mankind's great hope. Such a trust could not be forsaken; the future and happiness of untold millions depended on whether the nation could prove that democratic government was not " an absurdity." History had already proved that the people could successfully set up and operate such a government. But it had yet to show whether they could successfully resist a major effort to overthrow it. "We must settle this question now," Lincoln said, " whether in a free government the minority has the right to break up the government whenever they choose. If we fail it will go far to prove the incapability of the people to govern themselves."

That was why Lincoln resolved that the cause of the preservation of the Union must be fought for and won at all costs. The war put to the supreme test the liberal political ideal in America, and indeed, in western civilization, for the eyes of all Europe were on the United States. Would the greatest republic of the day come to an end? Would the government based upon the ideals of freedom and humanity succumb to a challenge affirming the good of slavery? Over and over again Lincoln stated these issues to the people, to the Congress, and to the world at large. Perhaps the best of these statements is the one Americans have come to know so well, the one they have taken to their hearts — the immortal Gettysburg speech. In the few minutes that it took him to say the 268 words, Lincoln summed up what America stood for and the significance of its tragic war: " a new nation, conceived in liberty and dedicated to the proposition that all men are created equal," and a trial in bloody civil strife to determine " whether that nation so conceived and so dedicated can long endure." Lincoln went on to say it was the responsibility of those who heard him on the scarred and rutted battlefield, and indeed, of all Americans of all generations in the future, to prove that this nation " under God shall have a new birth of freedom; and that government of the people, by the people, for the people shall not perish from the earth."

Lincoln's successful war leadership preserved the nation. During those four cruel years he was not without his critics who accused him of all kinds of mistakes, and even of more serious faults because of the measures he had at times to adopt. Some of these measures were hard, but Lincoln himself never was. As his biographer, Thomas has put it, " He exercised stern powers leniently, with regard for personal feelings and respect for human rights." It was as if Lincoln had become the embodiment of the liberal American, " easygoing and sentimental," personally revolting at extremes, but moving steadily, " if sometimes haltingly towards lofty goals."

Lincoln led the nation not only towards the goal of a reunited republic, based on charity and sympathy for the defeated South, but to the acceptance of the great principle of equality under the law. The war had been fought to preserve the Union, not to destroy slavery. But as the fighting went on it had become inevitable that slavery would be abolished. Here again Lincoln acted on the principle of reforming in order to preserve.

Death and martyrdom came to Lincoln before he had a chance to apply his great talents of liberal statesmanship to the enormous task that remained, the job of guiding the nation to a new unity. Peace had been won, but new hatreds were abroad in the land, and extremists were again challenging the tall gaunt man in the White House. Whether Lincoln would have had more success in healing the wounds of the war than those who followed him no one can say. We do know that the humane principles of " malice towards none and charity towards all " were not acceptable to the radicals in Lincoln's own party, some of whom actually characterized Lincoln's assassination as a " godsend to the country." But history has long since condemned the stupidity and shortsightedness of these small men, and has given to Lincoln the immortality that his achievements so well earned for him.

In Lincoln Americans see themselves and their striving for great liberal and humane causes. They renew their faith from Lincoln's faith; they strengthen their ideals from the example of his dedicated efforts to preserve and extend democratic government; they believe with him that freedom is indivisible and belongs to all mankind; and even more than in Lincoln's day, they hope, as he did, that in American democracy is the promise for the " progressive improvement in the condition of all men everywhere."

6

Henry David Thoreau

Samuel Middlebrook

Samuel Middlebrook, formerly an instructor at Marietta College, the University of Illinois, and New York University, is now associate professor of English at the College of the City of New York. For seven years he was associate editor of E. P. Dutton and Company. He is joint author of *The Eagle Screams* and co-editor of *English Literature and Its Backgrounds.*

Henry David Thoreau

Samuel Middlebrook

Liberal — derived from the Latin *liber*, a free man as opposed to a slave — is a word that changes color with each person who uses it. When capitalized it usually refers to a now dead political party of Great Britain whose most noted leader was Gladstone. In small letters it has always suggested some connection with *freedom*, some awareness of the untapped possibilities of man, and some variety of political, social, religious, or moral reform. History tells us that the reforms of any one generation never satisfy either that generation or its successors. Hence, liberalism, the battle cry of so many reformers, has to take on new meanings. Man is to have freedom, liberals say. But freedom *from* what? From want and fear? From too much government or tyranny, or too little government or anarchy? And freedom *for* what? For " manifest destiny " — a famous phrase that now suggests imperialism? The possibilities for argument are endless. Each great liberal in our American tradition seems to have his own special problems and answers.

In considering Thoreau, we are concerned with the problems and solutions of a small-town Massachusetts Yankee, whose one famous book was printed just over a century ago and has grown in reputation ever since. By general consent he is now considered a great American liberal. But what kind of liberal he was, what specific freedoms he sought for himself and others, what dangers he warned against, and how useful his ideas still are — all these are questions worthy of examination.

In doing this, we must look at the acts of this man Thoreau and his explanation of these acts; we must give thought to his life and writings.

Both are relatively short. He died at forty-five and he published only two books. The career of Thoreau illustrates the remark of his neighbor Emerson that great geniuses have the shortest biographies.

Thoreau was born in Concord, Massachusetts, in 1817. His family was moderately poor. They were pencil-makers by trade. With their help he worked his way through Harvard College, some fifteen miles distant. His class was that of 1837, the year when Emerson delivered his famous speech, "The American Scholar" to the Phi Beta Kappa Society of Harvard. Some students of our literature think that Emerson in this "intellectual declaration of independence," as it was called, really foretold the Thoreau of later years, for he defined the scholar to be "the Man Thinking" as opposed to the mere bookworm; the student who was cradled in nature, anxious for action, free and self-reliant, in contrast to the one who read great authors to feed his own inspiration. It is an interesting idea. The facts seem to be that Thoreau, like many of our writers who have gone to college, was an undistinguished undergraduate and not the Phi Beta Kappa type.

But a good class prophet of Harvard, 1837, could truly have declared that young Thoreau would become the man most likely to *secede*. Looked at from one angle, his life after Harvard was a series of brilliant withdrawals from the ordinary commitments of maturity. He withdrew from the official scholars of Harvard to his native town. Shortly afterward he withdrew from a venture of schoolteaching in Concord with a simple explanation: "As I did not teach for the good of my fellow-men but simply for a livelihood, this was a failure." He withdrew from Concord itself by building a shanty on Emerson's wood-lot at Walden pond; here he lived in partial seclusion for two years. He withdrew from this withdrawal by returning to town and living in Emerson's home as a kind of caretaker or very special "hired man." His most famous withdrawal is the time he seceded from the state of Massachusetts in 1845. His method was simple: he refused to pay his taxes. When the constable arrested him, on his way to have a pair of shoes mended at the local cobbler's, he calmly went to jail, prepared to rot there rather than pay a cent, even indirectly, toward the prosecution of an unjust war against Mexico. Legend has it that Emerson came to the jail and this conversation ensued:

" Henry, why are you here?"

" Waldo, why are you not here?"

There is no foundation for the legend except the temperament of the two men.

Thoreau had a theory that most men worked too long and too hard for too much. He preferred to alter the fourth commandment and labor one day a week, mostly at odd jobs like surveying, occasional pencil-making for the family, and leading others to patches of huckleberries. He was quietly mad about his home town: " I have travelled a good deal in Concord " was the way he put the matter. He claimed rightly that he knew the land thereabouts far better than did those who held the title deeds. Only a few times did he leave Concord after his Harvard days, a visit to Staten Island, trips on foot to the Maine Woods, to Cape Cod, to the White Mountains and Canada, and a final excursion to Minnesota in the year before his death. He died of tuberculosis in 1862, in his forty-fifth year. He met death with cheerfulness, for when an anxious friend inquired if he had made his peace with God he murmured: " I was not aware that we had ever quarreled."

To many of his acquaintances Thoreau must have seemed like a crank bent on wasting both his life and his education. He lived in the heyday of Jeffersonian democracy, when vast numbers of native Americans and new immigrants were streaming to our western plains or to our growing cities. California was available to gold-seekers; Kansas was available and bleeding for both frantic abolitionists and professional defenders of Negro slavery. Brook Farm, one of America's innumerable colonies for cooperative

Utopians, was almost next door to him at West Roxbury. Henry turned his back on all of these adventures. He stayed home and hoed beans. Beans, he knew from experience, were nutritious; and the stars that lighted his bean rows formed wonderful triangles. By contrast, the rewards of Brook Farm seemed very dubious.

It is a profound mistake to think of him as a hermit, however. He had astonishing neighbors and friends. Concord was small, but in creative ability it overflowed. Emerson, its acknowledged leading citizen, was both catalyst and magnet; he nourished the genius of the town's greatest native, Thoreau, and he attracted many other men of ability who, like himself, settled there. Hawthorne came there. So did Bronson Alcott, the inspired pedlar of Orphic ideas or the tedious archangel, depending on what day it was. Within Hawthorne's orbit was Herman Melville; within Emerson's was Walt Whitman, for Emerson was the first clear voice, apart from Whitman's own reviews of himself, to praise the *Leaves of Grass*. Concord, indeed, served as a source of inspiration to many of the outstanding literary figures of America.

To many of these writers Thoreau was a valued companion, though sometimes frightening. "I love Henry but I cannot like him," said a Concord friend, "and as for taking his arm, I should as soon think of taking the arm of an elm tree."

His own genius worked itself out, in his lifetime, chiefly in his second published book, *Walden*. This was an account of his two years in a shack on the shore of Walden pond, about three miles from the edge of town. He had gone there for the simplest of reasons: he wanted to think. A famous paragraph from the book gives the heart of the matter: "I went to the woods because I wished to live deliberately, to front only the essential facts of life, and see if I could not learn what it had to teach, and not, when I came to die, discover that I had not lived. I did not wish to live what was not life, living is so dear; nor did I wish to practise resignation, unless it was quite necessary. I wanted to live deep and suck out all the marrow of life, to live so sturdily and Spartan-like as to put to rout all that was not life, to cut a broad swath and shave close, to drive life into a corner, and reduce it to its lowest terms, and, if it proved mean, why then to get the whole and genuine meanness of it, and publish it to the world; or if it were sublime, to know it by experience, and be able to give a true account of it in my next excursion."

Sitting in a homemade cabin or shanty that had cost him $28.12½ in materials, Thoreau read a few books (such as the *Iliad* of Homer in Greek) when he felt like it. He wandered around the lake whenever he wished, chatted with townsfolk who came out to see him, watched birds and ants and trees, listened to train whistles, whippoorwills, distant cows, the cracking ice, and found that life, after all, could be a simple and sweet affair if a man would only have it so.

Steadfastly he peeled off the outer layers of experience like skins from an onion — and he discarded most of the skins. He was in search of grand simplicities, and he found many of them in terms of what he did not need. He didn't need meat or tobacco or wine or much companionship. (When asked what dish he preferred at dinner he replied: " The nearest.") He didn't need new clothes. He didn't need the gossip that makes up most daily papers or most conversations. He did not need the security that came from doing things for others that they could do better for themselves. Most of all he did not need the ownership of *things*.

On the other hand he did need — and found in the woods — three of the great liberalizing virtues. These were candor, courage, and faith in man. When a man has these virtues, and can illuminate them by one of the best prose styles in our literature, he is an enduring conscience for his countrymen.

Candor compelled him to look closely at Concord, which is of course only the world reduced to manageable limits. He described what he saw in an iron phrase: " The mass of men lead lives of quiet desperation." Ownership of useless things is one root of their troubles: they drag a house and sixty acres of dirt behind them to their graves. They hammer stone into useless shapes. They work, they worry over a hundred commercial ventures, ninety-seven of which turn out to be failures. They are fanatics, as the philosopher Santayana defined the term — " men who redouble their energies as they forget their aims." And if they happen to achieve what the world calls success, their bad conscience or their disordered bowels may lead them to inflict philanthropy and missionary enterprises upon their fellows.

It is a grim indictment that Thoreau presents. It is written as his personal challenge to his generation. We should not forget that it is also a young man's verdict on those in power around him. " I have lived some thirty years on this planet," he says, " and I have yet to hear the first syllable of valuable or even earnest advice from my seniors. . . . If I have any experience which I think valuable, I am sure to reflect that this my mentors said nothing about."

Having the candor to tell the truth as he saw it, Thoreau had also the courage to follow his own insights. He abandoned the approved goals of his society. He declined to save money though he insisted on paying his way. He made himself rich as Epicurus had taught, by making his wants small. He dissected the true aims of wealth into amusing simplicities. Thus, food is fuel to keep the body's fires alight. Clothing is an added shield of the flame. Shelter is a kind of immovable clothing. These are the essence of the matter; all refining of them is vanity. Harmless vanity perhaps, until the complications of providing for this vanity cost more than they bring in. And how shall we estimate the cost? Thoreau's formula, which we might call the first law of Transcendental Economics, is this: " The cost of a thing is the amount of what I will call *life* which is required to be exchanged for it, immediately or in the long run." As for himself, for most of the objects treasured by his neighbors and friends he declined to pay the price asked.

To protect his freedom he would keep only the slightest connection with an economic society.

So far as he was concerned, Thoreau was in earnest on this point. No profession or business that he might hold in Concord was worth the price it would cost him in terms of life. He declined to enter the "rat race." He would be a "sojourner in civilization," a spectator, not a competitor.

Being a spectator in Concord (or the world) was exciting business. For one thing, it let him see nature. "For many years," he says, "I was self-appointed inspector of snowstorms and rainstorms, and did my duty faithfully; surveyor if not of highways, then of forest paths and all across-lot routes. . . . I have looked after the wild stock of the town, which give a faithful herdsman a good deal of trouble by leaping fences: and I have had an eye to the unfrequented nooks and corners of the farm; though I did not always know whether Jonas or Solomon worked in a particular field today; that was none of my business."

Nature in the raw proved sometimes fierce. Thoreau once observed an epic battle between red and black ants, and picked up three fighters on a chip and watched them for an hour. The smaller red ants chewed the legs off a larger black one while he in turn beheaded them and staggered off with their heads still fastened to his vitals. The sight moved him as deeply as if he had watched in person the Revolutionary skirmish of Concord.

With Thoreau this sympathetic scrutiny of the non-human world brought him, as it did Wordsworth and other great romantics, back to human beings. A love of nature led to a renewed love of man — not man as he too often is, but man as he might be; man as the creator and creature of his own ideals; man as the dearly beloved son of God.

Not to see this point is to miss the essence of *Walden*. One can be put off by the mock-querulous tone of many of Thoreau's observations on his fellow men. Life is mean and ugly far too often.

But how do we know it to be mean? Do we not have a telltale instinct for something better? Let us trust this instinct, he says. Let us follow these impulses of the ideal world so mysteriously intermingled with our sorry present. Hence, the book, which begins with a striking epigram, " I have travelled a great deal in Concord," ends with a magnificent one, the best concluding sentence, I feel, in our whole nineteenth-century literature. It is this: " The sun is but a morning star."

In other words, the actualities of present-day life, even when they seem as fair as Venus in the sky before dawn, will fade before the glory of the future as the morning star fades in the radiance of the rising sun.

On this note of almost religious ecstasy, the book ends. Candor, courage, and faith in man, its three great points, must be the foundation stones of any enduring liberalism. Thoreau was of that New England generation that threw off the crushing first premise of Calvinism that man is a creature of total depravity: a worm, crushed and bleeding by the wayside; a loathsome spider held over the threatening fires of hell by the hand of an angry God — to use the famous phrase of that early Puritan, Jonathan Edwards.

Thoreau's gospel of faith in man is not fashionable in many intellectual circles today. The prophets of doom are once more upon us. Those who despise their fellow men can be found in the seats of the mighty. We have inquisitors, abroad and at home, who seem never to have heard Thoreau's quiet remark: " I think we may safely trust a good deal more than we do. . . . I foresee that all men will at length establish their lives on that basis." Such contemners, such inquisitors, despise heresy and are quick to detect it. How unlike they are from Thoreau with his shrewd comment: " If a man does not keep pace with his companions, perhaps it is because he hears a different drummer."

He did earn the active dislike of more worldly folk. James Russell Lowell, editor of the *Atlantic Monthly*, dismissed him as

a paradoxical eccentric. Robert Louis Stevenson found him a
" shirker." Both made these errors because they took him too
literally. This is easy to do. So vivid is the narrative of *Walden*,
so much of a Robinson Crusoe flavor attaches to his adventure of
building a house in the mild wilderness on the edge of Concord,
that some readers believe Thoreau advises them to imitate his actions literally. In freedom's name they should build their own
shanty, hoe their own beans, walk rather than ride, perhaps even
grow a beard, patch their own trousers and scorn the ballot box.
We have all seen such literal-minded " simple-lifers " even in the
busiest sections of our crowded cities. They do not arouse confidence. Often they do not even seem happy. Thoreau had en-
countered plenty of them in his own day, in which carefully cultivated eccentricity was common. His life was no pose; it was
simply and individually his own: " I should not talk so much about
myself," he says, " if there were anybody else whom I knew as
well." In this he implies that one should lead the life that his tru-
est impulses call him to lead.

The symbolic rather than literal nature of this book is disclosed
in an early paragraph: " I long ago lost a hound, a bay horse, and
a turtle-dove, and am still on their trail. Many are the travellers
I have spoken to concerning them, describing their tracks and
what calls they answered to. I have met one or two who had
heard the hound, and the tramp of the horse, and even seen the
dove disappear behind a cloud, and they seemed as anxious to re-
cover them as if they had lost them themselves."

What these mysterious beasts signify is anyone's guess. To me
they suggest Thoreau's ideals and the quest for them that he invites the like-minded to share.

In addition to his major book, *Walden*, he wrote an essay on
" Civil Disobedience," prompted by his brief stay in jail. In this
he advanced his notion that where the state clashed with the conscience of an individual, the individual should disown the state.
His withdrawal should be firm but non-violent. Probably many

have heard how Mahatma Gandhi, in 1907, found this essay, reprinted it in a magazine he then edited, and made it the basis of
his campaigns of nonviolence in India.   In this way, this quiet
Yankee had a hand in one of the most dramatic political events of
our age.

Never a " joiner," Thoreau did become active in the abolitionist movement.   He aided runaway slaves on the underground rail-
road.   He extravagantly admired John Brown, whom he had once
met in Concord two years before the raid on Harper's Ferry.   On
the day of Brown's execution in 1859, Thoreau tolled the bell at
the Concord meetinghouse and praised him as a martyr to liberty.
In a later mass meeting at Faneuil Hall in Boston he scorned a government that compromised with slavery.   He did not live to see
Gettysburg, the Emancipation Proclamation, and the work of
Abraham Lincoln.   By the time the Civil War broke out Thoreau
was a dying man.   He left behind an enormous journal, a sheaf of
articles, some of which had already been published, and letters and
poems, all of which expanded his writings to twenty volumes.

Yet, except for specialists, he remains a man of one book.
Walden contains his deepest insights, his most telling phrases, his
most valuable self-portrait.   It has gained in stature and ranks
with Whitman's *Leaves of Grass* or Emerson's *Essays* as one of
the great documents of American liberalism.

In our day of enormous cities, mass organizations of labor and
capital, syndicated newspaper columns, radio networks, central-
ized governments and conscription, it is easy to find Thoreau's
liberalism one-sided.   Man seems organized as never before — for
getting born, for an education, for a job, for being investigated,
even for an obituary, which is usually a record of the clubs, com-
panies and associations that one has belonged to.   The individual
seems less and less; the group seems more and more.

For this group side of human life Thoreau manifested complete
indifference.   Let others write or think of it, he seems to say.   Society, like gravitation, will hold us all by a force that never re-

laxes. There must, however, be a counterforce to keep us in our orbit, or we shall all be piled up into a heap of faceless anonymities.

Thoreau's life and writing were an example of this counterforce at work. For him the test of any society was the individuals therein. Was each one *himself*, sacred and irreplaceable and above all responsible for his own ideals? One must work out these ideals for himself, Thoreau believed. No one else can do the job. The task requires all of one's candor, all of one's courage; and all of one's faith in man — the faith that moved Socrates when condemned to death by the Athenians, to say: " The unexamined life is not worth living." Thoreau chose Walden as the place where he could examine his life. And we too as American liberals have to find our own Walden.

7
Walt Whitman

Elias Lieberman

Elias Lieberman, who in 1954 retired as associate superintendent of schools of New York City, had formerly been principal of the Thomas Jefferson High School, Brooklyn. He has served as editor of *Puck*, literary editor of *The American Hebrew*, and contributing editor of *Current Literature*. Among his books are *The American Short Story; Poetry for Junior High Schools; Poems for Enjoyment;* and four collections of his own verse.

Walt Whitman

Elias Lieberman

"He is democracy," said Thoreau after a visit to Walt Whitman in 1856. Although he voiced his objection to the sensuality of the *Leaves of Grass* in a letter to a friend, Thoreau stated: " He [Whitman] is apparently the greatest Democrat the world has ever seen. . . . I have just read his second edition (which he gave me) and it has done me more good than any reading for a long time. . . . I do not believe that all the sermons so called that have been preached in this land put together are equal to it for preaching."

Thoreau was one of the few understanding spirits of Whitman's own time who recognized *Leaves of Grass* as a unique expression of democracy. It took almost three quarters of a century before *Leaves of Grass* became the symbol of democracy not only in the United States but also throughout the world. It has been translated into many languages, among them Danish, Japanese, and Hebrew. Some of the poems seem to have been written for the twentieth century to hearten fighters in the resistance movements against totalitarianism. In the form and substance of American poetry Whitman was a liberator; in his concept of democracy he was a seer and a guide.

The impact of Walt Whitman on American poetry came like a delayed action bomb followed by a mild earthquake. For a long time after the first edition of *Leaves of Grass* appeared in 1855 Walt Whitman's poetry was either ignored or reviled. At best it was damned with the faintest of faint praise by critics too well aware of the social unpopularity of the author. Only Emerson had the courage and the critical acumen to grasp the fact that with *Leaves of Grass* a great original talent was making itself felt.

He wrote to Whitman after he had read the gift copy which Whitman sent him, "I give you joy of your free and brave thought. I have great joy in it. . . . I find the courage of treatment which so delights us and which large perception only can inspire. I greet you at the beginning of a great career."

When I was a little boy attending elementary school I often gazed at a panel of American poets displayed in the school's assembly hall. Among the poets who were then regarded as foremost were Longfellow, Whittier, Lowell, Bryant, and Joaquin Miller. Two significant omissions at this time — the last decade of the nineteenth century — were Edgar Allan Poe and Walt Whitman. Any critic today would be regarded as unworthy of his important function if he chose to overlook the influence and achievements of both these men whom it was fashionable then either to slight entirely or to accept with apologetic reservations. Strangely enough it was well known even then to those who had knowledge of world literature that both Poe and Whitman were not only greatly admired in Europe but that they were leaving their impress on schools of writers anxious to free themselves from the trammels of a sterile sort of classicism. The restrictions of matter and manner imposed upon artists by the French Royal Academy of Fine Arts brought on a similar rebellion of painters in the early decades of the nineteenth century.

It is not an exaggeration to point out that in the renaissance of poetry, which started in our country about 1912 with the first issue of Harriet Monroe's poetry magazine, the influence of Walt Whitman played a dominant part. The revolt against the too decorous and too regular verses with little new to say, as exemplified in the works of Edmund C. Stedman, Richard Watson Gilder and, on a little lower plane of sentimentality, Ella Wheeler Wilcox, was led by such Whitman enthusiasts as Carl Sandburg, Vachel Lindsay, Edgar Lee Masters, and James Oppenheim. Their own formidable talents would not have been fully developed had they not accepted the liberating influence of Whitman.

Brander Matthews, who as a critic tried to be fair to Whitman, nevertheless wrote in *A Study of Versification*, " It may be well to mention also that the principle that the accord shall be on the vowel of the final long syllable is violated by Walt Whitman who mates *exulting* and *daring, crowding* and *turning* and by Poe who conjoins *dead* and *tenanted*." Today these usages are accepted by modern poets aware of the paucity of rhyming words in English, thanks to the pioneer experiments of both Poe and Whitman. Of the Whitman themes, which represented an even greater break with tradition than his forms, it must be conceded that such poems as *The Widow in the Bye Street* by Masefield and *The Bridge* by Hart Crane, to take two examples from different literary eras, were influenced in their realism by Walt Whitman who defended the

. . . devilish and the dark, the dying and diseased
The countless (nineteen twentieths) low and evil, crude and savage,
The crazed prisoners in jail, the horrible, rank, malignant,
Venom and filth, serpents, the ravenous sharks, liars, the dissolute.

This was Whitman's way of affirming John Keats' famous lines,

> Beauty is truth, truth, beauty, that is all
> Ye know on earth and all ye need to know,

the couplet which artistically concludes his " Ode on a Grecian Urn." The thrill of glimpsing the truth, both poets believed, is akin to a vision of the beautiful. It is upon this broad principle that so much modern work both in the novel and in poetry is based.

Like the lives of other poets Whitman's was a constant struggle for self-realization. His early background is a study in experimental groping. Whitman was born in 1819, ten years after Edgar Allan Poe, but when Poe died in 1849 Whitman had not yet issued the first edition of the *Leaves of Grass*. Whitman's mother was of Dutch Quaker descent; his father, of English Puritan stock, farmers mainly who tilled American soil for more than 150 years.

Whitman was born at West Hills near Huntington, Long Island, but the family soon moved to Brooklyn. It was there in an elementary school that he learned the rudiments of the three R's but left school before he reached his teens. At 11 he was an errand boy, at 12 a " printer's devil," at 14 a typesetter in the composing room of The Long Island *Star*, and at 17 an itinerant printer-journalist in the city of New York. Except for the fact that the boy was intelligent and able to make up his own incomplete schooling to the extent of being himself able and willing to teach school at the age of 17, there is no evidence at this point in his career that he had a dynamic and original mind. In addition to teaching at this stage — so low was the estate of pedagogy — he also delivered papers and contributed " pieces " to the Long Island *Democrat*. Maybe there is a hint of his own future in the name of the paper he chose to write for. His love of printer's ink must have been authentic even then, because when he returned to Brooklyn and New York in 1841 he busied himself with miscellaneous literary chores such as writing fillers, short stories, a novelette, verses, and editorials. His first steady editorial position was on the Brooklyn *Evening Star*, which he left to become editor of the Brooklyn *Daily Eagle* in 1846.

A considerable body of Whitman's editorials and reviews for these newspapers has been reprinted. In them the young editor dealt with the political problems of the day. It was the time that a war with Mexico threatened, a dispute with Oregon broke out, and the issues of free trade and the extension of slavery were being hotly debated. On most of these issues Whitman vigorously expressed himself, taking the stand of the Democratic party. On the issue of free soil he sided so emphatically with the more radical faction of the party, the so-called Barnburners, that he lost his job with the *Eagle*, after almost two years of remarkable success in the position of editor.

In addition to political and civic affairs Whitman wrote about such social matters as prison reform and child and female labor.

His views on civic and humanitarian problems were often far in advance of his time. Of considerable interest today are his articles on education and the schools, published in Florence Bernstein Freedman's *Walt Whitman Looks at the Schools*. For example, in one of his contributions to the Brooklyn *Evening Star* he has this to say about current school practices: " A ridiculous and vexatious rule prevails in our Brooklyn schools, by which every scholar is required to furnish his or her books, paper etc. . . . It is a miserable, petty economy that deserves to be scouted and hooted at till it is reformed." There is something of the Whitman fire in these lines.

Corporal punishment infuriated Whitman. In the same editorial he wrote: " A teacher who pursues this practice shows himself to be unfit for his office; if he cannot govern a flock of boys and girls without the rattan and the ferule, he should never be placed over them." Whitman's views on the personality of teachers would please those charged with the responsibility of licensing only the fit and meritorious. Whitman preached:

We would recommend also the much more frequent and general employment of lady-like and well-educated women as teachers of youth. The refinement of the female character, and its mildness, its natural sympathy with the feelings of children and its instinctive knowledge of the best avenues to their obedience and good will recommend them invariably as the best teachers. Nor are we saying too much here. If boys were more generally brought under the gentle potency of female polish, how few would be those awkward gaukeys, those blustering ill-favored juvenile rowdies that swarm now in every street.

This does not sound at all like a barbaric yawp.

Whitman comes close to John Dewey in his estimate of the potentialities of children when he writes on March 6, 1846, in the *Evening Star:* " It is strange that many people can never be fond of boys and girls. What are their little faults but the trivial weakness of a moment? And who that has the least tact cannot draw out some interesting phase from what are called spoilt and dis-

agreeable children? If a child is not engaging while you have in-
tercourse with him it is your fault. His mind and conversation
are as a mirror which reflects the aspect of your own. God makes
no human creature without some beautiful qualities. . . ." Whitman then attacks " the artificial and false conventionalities of society " that strive to crush " the fresh impulses of the natural
mind " and ends by asserting — he is beginning to emerge as the
Yea Sayer, the affirmative force in a muddled world — that even
then " enough of the divine heritage remains always to respond to
the kindred divinity of love, truth and sweet offices." Whitman
points out under the caption " Absurdities in School Government," after he has deplored practices in certain public schools in
Brooklyn " where children are used as so many automata," that
the " object of true schools is to teach the children." Then he
goes on to say, " all forms and rules are mere shadows, only substantial inasmuch as they aid the other, — To elevate the mind of
a child, to spur it on with words of cheer and encouragement, to
open by kindness, gentleness and firmness its own rich stores,
these are the things to aim after. Mere rote or book learning is a
very little part of education, after all. And these thumping drill-
ing teachers are at the very porch of learning themselves and are
not fit for their station."

No champion of modified, progressive education, which stresses
the unfolding of a child's personality through purposeful activities, could have put the case for the psychological approach more
eloquently. Here is a divine creation, the child, Whitman is saying; do not spoil him by turning him into a robot, a mere machine, by your numerous restrictions and " rigid forms."

In many respects the career of Whitman the journalist was a
curtain raiser for the career of Whitman the poet. He was in favor of immigration, writing, " How, then, can any man with a
heart in his breast, begrudge the coming of Europe's needy ones
to the plentiful storehouse of the new world? " Although Whitman was never an ardent abolitionist, putting the preservation of

the union ahead of the issue of slavery, he was adamant in his insistence that slavery should not come into new territory. In his later poetry he drew an unforgettable sketch of the runaway slave:

The runaway slave came to my house and stopt outside,
I heard his motions crackling the twigs of the woodpile,
Through the swung half-door of the kitchen I saw him limpsy and weak,
And went where he sat on a log and led him in and assured him,
And brought water and filled a tub for his sweated body and bruis'd feet,
And gave him a room that entered from my own, and gave him some coarse clean clothes.
. . . .
He staid with me a week before he was recuperated and pass'd North,
I had him sit next me at table, my fire-lock leaned in the corner.

Five years before *Leaves of Grass* appeared, Whitman at the age of thirty-one began assuming the Whitmanesque pose associated with his name today. He discarded the somewhat dandified clothing to which he had been partial and began wearing the clothes of a workman. It was then that he started to consort with " powerful uneducated persons " — ferry men, bus drivers, roustabouts along the wharves and docks. Many legends about Whitman have their origins during this period when young manhood was ending and the fulfilment of his career became a violent urge. It is said, for example, that on one occasion he drove a bus and shouted passages from Shakespeare; on another, that he was overheard reading from Epictetus to a boatman. His poems were shaping up as reflections of realities and not as polite mirages of an academic past. During that period there was plenty of room in his consciousness for Shakespeare, Epictetus, bus drivers, and boatmen. Whitman was trying hard to understand the strange world beyond the parlors of the literati — a world in which good and evil are inextricably mixed.

The attempt on the part of Whitman to reconcile true worth with the accidentals of external appearances led him to seek fitting forms for the expression of his ideas. Obviously the ticktock of regular iambics and the constriction of perfect rhyming were obstacles in projecting powerfully his divergent images of freedom and his sense of the magnetic unity which gave human diversity its deepest meaning under God. His declaration of independence from classical backgrounds, hackneyed themes, and foreign influences is well stated in this passage from " Song of the Exposition ":

Come, Muse, migrate from Greece and Ionia,
Cross out please those immensely overpaid accounts,
That matter of Troy and Achilles' wrath and Aeneas', Odysseus'
    wanderings,
Placard " Removed " and " To Let " on the rocks of your snowy
    Parnassus,
Repeat at Jerusalem, place the notice high on Jaffa's gate and on
    Mount Moriah,
The same on the walls of your German, French and Spanish castles
    and Italian collections,
For know a better, fresher, busier sphere, a wide, untried domain
    awaits you.

Naturally this new approach to poetry in Whitman's plan was vitally connected with the democratic recognition of " the common man." It was Wordsworth who only a few decades before Whitman enunciated the beauty hidden in the seemingly commonplace. Whitman glorified as God's masterpieces the men in the street and in the factories, the humblest men and women in the lowliest environments. His version of our national motto, " E Pluribus Unum," was expressed in the lines entitled " I Hear America Singing ":

I hear America singing, the varied carols I hear,
Those of mechanics each one singing his as it should be, blithe and
    strong,

The carpenter singing his as he measures his plank or beam,
The mason singing his as he makes ready for work, or leaves off work,
The boatman singing what belongs to him in his boat, the deckhand
　singing on the steamboat deck,
The shoemaker singing as he sits on his bench, the hatter singing as he
　stands,
The woodcutter's song, the plowboy's on his way in the morning, or
　at noon intermission or at sundown,
Each singing what belongs to the day — at night the party of young
　fellows, robust, friendly,
Singing with open mouths their strong melodious songs.

It is Whitman's identification of himself with all people and
with all scenes, with good and with evil, with the noble and the
base, which explains his intensity and the lapses from good taste
for which he had been criticized. These, however, must be regarded as excesses of his missionary zeal, the extremes which inevitably accompany the launching of a new movement and which
time modifies. His " Song of Myself " explains much if the reader
is prepared to journey through material that is unrestrained and
repetitious. A few lines from this poem are sufficient to highlight
what Whitman most wished to say:

I celebrate myself and sing myself,
And what I assume you shall assume,
For every atom belonging to me as good belongs to you.
I loafe and invite my soul,
I learn and loafe at my ease observing a spear of summer grass.
Stop this day and night with me and you shall possess the origins of
　all poems. . . .

Leaves of Grass in its first edition contained only 12 poems and
was brought out anonymously; the second edition, published a
year later, in 1856, contained 32 poems and the third, published in
1860, included 157 poems. In a sense, throughout the rest of his
life Whitman was issuing editions of *Leaves of Grass,* compre-

hending all of his later work in poetry under this inspired title. In his poems, in the prefaces to some of the editions, and in his prose works Whitman expressed his philosophy of democracy as well as his reactions to people, ideas, and to the world of nature.

It was the Civil War, and particularly its great and tragic figure, Abraham Lincoln, which finally matured and intensified the poetic genius of Walt Whitman. When the war between the states broke out Whitman did not enlist but his brother George did. Whitman, however, soon found in the dramatic struggle a role that was consistent with his humanitarian aims and philosophy. When George was wounded, Walt undertook the task of nursing him. He then remained in Washington, helping and serving in the hospitals. He performed all the tasks he could for disabled men, writing their letters for them, bringing them ice cream and tobacco, and often reading to them various tales and poems.

Whitman's firsthand experiences were recorded in his collection, *Drum Taps*, which later became part of *Leaves of Grass*. Two of his noblest poems had their origins in his unquenchable grief at the assassination of Abraham Lincoln. These represent Whitman at his very best. The blustering, posing champion of virility and of the natural life revealed deep tenderness as well as accomplished artistry in " Come up from the Fields, Father " which shows the impact of war in terms of the suffering it imposed upon people and in " When Lilacs Last in the Dooryard Bloomed," the ultimate expression and the essence of the grief which seized so many people when Abraham Lincoln was murdered and a bewildered country found itself leaderless. Although this poem is a poignant song of death, of mourning, the sprig of lilac laid on the coffin is a symbol of life everlasting.

The Civil War taught Whitman a profound lesson. He learned to know and to understand soldiers from all parts of the United States. After the war he really became the poet of the whole country and extended his vision to include the universe. He understood now the " en masse " of which he had written. He also became more realistic in his view of democracy as it then expressed itself in customs and institutions.

His vision of the ideal democracy never faltered. In *Democratic Vistas*, an essay published in 1871 simultaneously with the fifth edition of *Leaves of Grass*, Whitman repeatedly indicted the falsities and shortcomings of American democracy in his time. He said in part:

. . . society in these states is canker'd, crude, superstitious, and rotten. . . . Never was there, perhaps, more hollowness at heart than at present, and here in the United States. . . . The depravity of the business classes is not less than has been supposed but infinitely greater. The official services of America, national, state and municipal, in all their branches and departments except the judiciary, are saturated in corruption, bribery, falsehood and mal-administration, and the judiciary is tainted. . . . It is as if somehow we were being endow'd with a vast and more and more thoroughly-appointed body, and then left with little or no soul.

Yet he did not despair of democracy. "Democracy is a great word, whose history, I suppose, remains unwritten, because the history has yet to be enacted." He maintained his faith in the United States. In 1888, toward the end of his life, casting backward glances over the road he had traveled, Whitman wrote: "One main genesis-motive of the *Leaves* was my conviction (just as strong today as ever) that the crowning growth of the United States is to be spiritual and heroic."

In the very year in which Whitman deplored the shortcomings of American democracy in *Democratic Vistas*, he wrote *Passage to India*, a poem which he said contained more of himself than any other. In it he envisioned unity among nations as democracy advanced throughout the world:

Passage to India!
Lo, soul, seest thou not God's purpose from the first?
The earth to be spann'd, connected by network,

The races, neighbors, to marry and be given in marriage,
The oceans to be cross'd, the distant brought near,
The lands to be welded together.

It almost seems as if there is an adumbration of the United Nations in his " Years of the Modern ":

What whispers are these O lands, running ahead of you, passing under the seas?
Are all nations communing? is there going to be but one heart to the globe?
Is humanity forming en masse? for lo, tyrants tremble, crowns grow dim,
The earth, restive, confronts a new era. . . .
. . . .
Your dreams O years, how they penetrate through me. (I know not whether I sleep or wake;)
The perform'd America and Europe grow dim, retiring in the shadow behind me.
The unperform'd, more gigantic than ever, advance, advance upon me.

The question may well be asked: to what extent did Whitman open the door to that new era? Writers have acknowledged their debt to him. Robert Louis Stevenson, for example, wrote of *Leaves of Grass* in 1887: "A book of singular service, a book which tumbled the world upside down for me, blew into space a thousand cobwebs of genteel and ethical illusion, and, having thus shaken my tabernacle of lies, set me back again upon a strong foundation. . . . But it is only a book for those who have the gift of reading."

Not only was the style of modern poetry influenced by Whitman but also choice of content. His " To a Locomotive in Winter " projected machinery as a subject for poetry and also aspects of science. Joseph Beaver in his recent book, *Walt Whitman, Poet of Science*, calls him " the first American poet to embody modern scientific concepts in his work in a poetic manner " and contends that in matters of science Whitman was more consistent and better informed than has been supposed.

It is more difficult to trace Whitman's influence on the growth and spread of the democratic ideal, although such influence does exist throughout the world. Studies of parallels between his ideas and those of modern poets and novelists and liberal thinkers have shown marked similarities too strong to be merely coincidental. One oblique but direct contribution of Whitman to the liberal spirit was his influence on the declaration embodying the Fourteen Points. General Smuts, who is said to have been largely responsible for the Fourteen Points, was a Whitman enthusiast, even to the extent of writing a book about him. In 1915 Van Wyck Brooks wrote in *America's Coming of Age:* " Every strong personal impulse, everything that enriches the social background, everything that impels and clarifies in the modern world owes something to Walt Whitman."

Walt Whitman once claimed that his book was a candidate for the future. The summing up of all available evidence would seem to indicate that the future may well have been shaped in part by that very book.

Whitman, like Abraham Lincoln, throughout his tempestuous life suffered from abuse and misunderstanding. He bore his suffering manfully, overcoming even the crippling effects of a paralytic stroke because like Lincoln he willed to keep his course as a liberal straight toward his objective. Like Lincoln too, now that his work and his influence can be seen in perspective, he belongs to the ages.

8

Susan B. Anthony

Isidore Starr

Isidore Starr, instructor of social studies at Brooklyn Technical High School and a member of the New York Bar, is on the executive board of *Social Education*, the official publication of the National Council for Social Studies. A recipient of the John Hay Fellowship in the humanities, he is the author of *Human Rights in the United States*.

Susan B. Anthony

Isidore Starr

There is a sentence in our Constitution which reads: " The right of citizens of the United States to vote shall not be denied or abridged by the United States or by any State *on account of sex.*"

These words cast a long shadow. And as we peer into their historic past we discern the dominating image of Miss Susan B. Anthony, a great American, who died almost half a century ago, but whose spirit still lives in the liberal institutions of American political life.

The liberal analyzes and questions the status quo, the habit-patterns which cake society. Critical of *what is,* he is always searching, thinking and fighting for *what ought to be.* He doesn't want society stood on its head; he wants society reformed so that all men and women may be partners in the adventure of living together and creating a better world.

Such a liberal — and such a woman — was Susan Brownell Anthony. She loved liberty, equality, and social justice for all people. Her devotion to humanity transcended class, color, race, religion, and sex. And most important of all, she was endowed with a remarkable mind of her own — a factor which was to prove most disturbing to the society in which she lived.

When Susan was quite young she heard her teacher say: " The girls of the nineteenth century must behave precisely as the girls have behaved in all the other centuries. . . . The sanctity of tradition must be always upheld." But Susan asked herself " why? " and she concluded that not all traditions were best for society. This began the great tug of war.

What were the designs that entered into the pattern of her liberalism? What led her to spend the eighty-six years of her life in a Spartan-like devotion to studying and seeking to solve the burning issues of her time — temperance, slavery, and women's rights?

Her closest friend, Elizabeth Cady Stanton, had this to say about her: " In ancient Greece she would have been a Stoic; in the era of the Reformation, a Calvinist; in King Charles' time, a Puritan; but in this nineteenth century, by the very laws of her being, she is a reformer." Perhaps this is as good an explanation as any. She was born with that mystical and unique spark which separates the reformer from the conformer.

The first thirty years of Susan's life constituted one of the most unusual periods in our history — the Age of Jacksonian Democracy. It was an era distinguished for its idealistic ferment, its intellectual unrest, and its quest for social justice. All this struck a responsive chord in Susan, and it generated in her the need for participating in the upsurging humanitarianism of her time.

Unquestionably her unusual parents played a dominant role in keeping the flame of liberalism alive. The father was an independent, one might even say a rebellious Quaker, and the mother was a very sensitive Baptist. Together they created a home atmosphere characterized by moral zeal and respect for individual freedom, even for women. Their Rochester home became the meeting place of such distinguished crusaders as William Lloyd Garrison, Wendell Phillips, and Frederick Douglass. Susan got to know these men personally, and the spark with which she was born was nurtured by their friendship.

Perhaps all these influences — the inner self, the parents, and the example of important men — help to explain why she consecrated her life to reform and why she found in the woman suffrage movement an outlet for her emotions, her religious beliefs, and her social philosophy.

Teaching in the public schools of Rochester, New York, she received $8 a month as compared with the $25 and $30 which men were paid for the same type of work. This vexed her particularly because on one occasion she was given a job in a country school where the previous teacher, a man, had been literally forced out of the classroom by as rowdy a group of teacher-baiting students as any harassed instructor ever faced. Where the man had failed, Susan succeeded. This gentle Quaker girl picked out the leader of the louts, rolled up her sleeves, selected a sturdy birch rod, and — as her closest friend described the incident — resorted to the *argumentum ad hominem* by demonstrating the *a posteriori* method of reasoning. For this achievement she won the highest accolade that man could confer on woman. Said one of the males in the community: "By gosh, this woman's got the nerve of a man," and that was true.

She never lacked this nerve throughout her life. It was during her fifteen years as a successful teacher that she demanded equal pay for equal work for all teachers. She became an important figure at meetings of the New York State Teachers Association, where she kept offering petitions and resolutions demanding for women all the privileges enjoyed by men. In addition, she fought discrimination against Negro teachers and children in the public schools. She was also interested in coeducation and equality for both sexes in all schools, colleges, and universities.

It was at the age of thirty that Miss Anthony began really publicly to advocate her ideas of reform. The issue was "Demon Rum."

Among the customs which the colonists had imported from England was that of tippling; the Americans almost immediately improved on this practice by inventing a native whiskey and applejack. In a world characterized by Puritanical restrictions on gaiety, recreation was eagerly sought, and very often found, in drink. To the evil of the saloon was added the amazing capacity of the nineteenth-century male for liquor. It was not unusual for two bottles of wine per guest to be considered mere appetizers to the real liquid refreshment.

The victims of drunkenness were not only men but their wives and children as well. The temperance movement, aware of the crimes and sufferings resulting from the use of liquor, sought to stop its sale.

Miss Anthony, as a delegate to a meeting held by the Sons of Temperance in Albany, tried to gain the floor and speak on a motion, but she was quickly informed that sisters were there to be seen, to listen and to learn, but not to be heard. She replied, in her characteristic fashion, by helping to organize the Women's State Temperance Society of New York, the first of its kind.

But the opposition to women's participation in public affairs was overwhelming, and at times, even violent. Susan became increasingly convinced that only through equal rights could women develop into effective workers for social betterment.

Her work in the temperance movement paved her way as a reformer in the anti-slavery crusade. In the 1850's Miss Anthony worked for the American Anti-Slavery Society. This was not surprising, as the reformers of this period were involved both in the temperance and in the anti-slavery movements. However, she took the radical abolitionist stand and campaigned under the banner, " No union with slaveholders! " It took great courage in those days — as it takes today — to espouse an unpopular cause, and, as was to be expected, she met the usual fate. There were the howling hooligans and the rambunctious rowdies; there were jeers, groans, rotten eggs, and burning effigies. But she stood her ground like a man!

After the Civil War Miss Anthony was one of the first to advocate Negro suffrage. At the same time she fought to have included in the Fourteenth Amendment a provision giving the vote to women as well as to male Negroes. When this Amendment as passed introduced into the Constitution for the first time the word " male," she exploded and refused to go along with those who believed that this should be the Negro's hour. She wanted the word " male " dropped, for she felt that in this way both Negroes and women would win the right to vote. With this defeat came the resolve to dedicate her life to the one reform which could give women the same sense of dignity possessed by men — the right to vote and thereby to determine their political, economic, and social status.

Susan B. Anthony was what one might call a fine figure of a woman, with a face " lighted with the spiritual beauty which lifelong devotion to high purpose often imparts." One of her marriage proposals came from a rich dairy farmer, who appraised her as one who could do a good job milking his sixty cows.

She had several offers of matrimony, but she refused to marry and become a man's legalized servant. Her argument was that she could not consent that the man she loved, described in the Constitution as a white, male, native-born, American citizen, possessed of the right of self-government, eligible to the office of President of the great Republic, should unite his destinies in marriage with a political slave and pariah. " No, no," she exclaimed, " when I am crowned with all the rights, privileges, and immunities of a citizen, I may give some consideration to these special problems; but until then I must concentrate all my energies on the enfranchisement of my own sex."

It is interesting to note what was the legal relationship between the sexes in the mid-nineteenth century. Certainly, for women, especially the sensitive ones, many of the practices of this period seemed the offspring of social prejudice and bigotry. In general, most educational institutions were closed to them; few means of gainful employment were available; their earnings and their property belonged to their husbands; and fathers legally controlled the destinies of their children. In short, it seemed that woman was virtually the property of her male relations.

One of the most important reasons for this general acceptance of female inferiority was the fact that American law was based on the English common law. The impressive figure of Sir William Blackstone, conservative British jurist, hovered over our lawyers and lawmakers. For Blackstone, a woman civilly married was a woman civilly dead, a principle which was stated in the American law of the time as follows: " In marriage, man and woman become one, and that one is the husband."

This Quaker girl, who had never before used the ballot, believed that only through the achievement of the most important of democratic weapons — political suffrage — could woman wipe out her disabilities and gain for herself the dignified place to which she was rightfully entitled.

The half-century during which Susan B. Anthony was in the forefront of the fight for woman suffrage represents a case study of a great liberal in action. It shows how an extraordinary personality can by persistent pressure leave an indelible impression on that slow-moving mass that we call society.

First, she used her remarkable physical endurance to travel all over our country educating all she met with the importance of her cause. Here is a brief note from her diary on the last day of 1871:

Left Medicine Bow at noon, went through deep snow cuts ten feet in length. . . . Reached Laramie at ten P.M. Thus closes 1871, a year full of hard work, six months east, six months west of the Rocky Mountains; 171 lectures, 13,000 miles of travel; gross receipts, $4,318, paid on debts $2,271. Nothing ahead but to plod on.

Barns, lyceums, lumber wagons, open air gatherings, even saloons were the platforms and forums for her views. And so also were the fashionable gatherings at Saratoga Springs. Twice she traveled to Europe — the second time at the age of eighty-four to attend the International Congresses of Women in London and in Berlin.

No personal sacrifice was too great, no discomfort too difficult for her cause. Susan B. Anthony traveled so that she could carry the message of woman suffrage everywhere. Lecturing five and six times a week when the occasion demanded, often substituting for speakers who failed to appear, she never hesitated to face an audience — even those dominated by that lunatic fringe which vents its spleen with hisses, overripe tomatoes, and vile and obscene clamor. Late in life, she couldn't help reminiscing before a large and enthusiastic audience: " Time brings strange changes. In this very city that has pelted me with roses I have been pelted with rotten eggs for saying the very things that I have said tonight."

Susan B. Anthony became a familiar figure at legislative committee hearings. In New York she pleaded for liberalization of the laws relating to a married woman's earnings and the guardianship of her children. In Washington she fought year after year for the greatest prize of all — an amendment to the Constitution. She kept trying to get woman suffrage planks into the Democratic and Republican platforms — but all she obtained were " splinters."

She set aside time for correspondence with influential people, and for the publication over a period of two years of a weekly journal, *The Revolution*. Many a complacent citizen must have been regularly ruffled by the defiant tone and slogan of this periodical which proclaimed: " Men, their rights and nothing more; Women, their rights and nothing less! "

But that was not all. Miss Anthony found it necessary to write *A History of Woman Suffrage* to summarize the achievements as well as the unfinished business of this great movement. Together with Elizabeth Cady Stanton and Mathilda Joslyn Gage she started a multi-volume repository of all the significant data which would help to educate and to enlighten the public.

All this work was significant and impressive. But we have not as yet touched upon her greatest activity — that which must serve as an object lesson to all liberals.

There comes a time in every great reform movement when the days seem very dark, the obstacles too numerous, the defeats most discouraging. There comes a time when the prima donnas in the campaign — the superb speakers and the gifted writers — having played their parts, leave the stage. There comes a time when a reform movement hovers on the brink of history's limbo. At this point in the movement to enfranchise women, Susan B. Anthony made her greatest contribution. Talk about reform was complemented with action for political change.

Marshaling every available weapon at her command, she attacked at all points: state legislatures, territorial governments, and Congress. She did not let anyone forget the ideal for which she was fighting — an amendment to the Constitution.

But there always remained the innumerable and endless minute details — the stubborn facts that have to be faced and handled to keep a movement alive from day to day. She was not only a great organizer, master tactician and leader; she was also the director of daily activities. Money had to be raised, speakers mobilized, conventions arranged, petitions signed, resolutions presented to the proper agencies. All this she did — with others when possible, alone when necessary.

Her superb skill in planning and managing was best seen in the creation of associations which became focal centers of widespread activity. When the Sons of Temperance seemed inadequate, she created the Woman's State Temperance Society of New York. Then came the American Equal Rights Association, followed by the National Woman Suffrage Association which was formed to secure an amendment to the Federal Constitution. In 1890 the more radical wing of the movement, led by Susan B. Anthony and Elizabeth Cady Stanton, merged with the more conservative group, which had advocated state action as the better solution. The newly organized National American Woman Suffrage Association honored Miss Anthony with the presidency from 1892 to 1900, at which time she voluntarily retired.

Anyone who dedicates himself — or herself — to a public cause must be prepared for the entire spectrum of critical appraisal. Anyone who deals in public controversy knows that the very taking of a positive stand evokes the mixed chorus of applause, derogation, and belittlement.

Susan B. Anthony, during her long life, did much that aroused such sharp differences of opinion. Consider the following two incidents.

In the 1850's Amelia Bloomer and others, including Miss Anthony, introduced a new note in women's fashions: the famous Bloomer costume of short skirt and Turkish trousers. Designed to "sensationalize the men out of their fossilized prejudices," it produced results which any man could foresee, but which the feminists never anticipated. That the men were at once attracted was inevitable, but their attention most certainly was not drawn to the intellectual issues involved. One year of this bifurcated costume was enough for Miss Anthony and she abandoned it with this comment: " I found it a physical comfort but a mental crucifixion. The attention of my audience was fixed upon my clothes instead of my words. I learned the lesson then that to be successful a person must attempt but one reform."

The second incident is the important story behind the seemingly impersonal judicial note: *United States* v. *Susan B. Anthony.* Believing that the Fourteenth Amendment entitled women to the right to vote, Miss Anthony registered with fifteen other women and voted in the presidential election of 1872. Arrested for illegal voting, she was released on bail. While awaiting trial, she undertook a series of public lectures to educate every potential juror on the issues of the case. When the Attorney General succeeded in gaining a change of venue, she began a second campaign of juror education. However, the judge refused to give the case to the jury, delivered an opinion reportedly written before the trial had taken place, and directed the jury to bring in a verdict of guilty. The fine of $100 she simply refused to pay and it was never paid. Her philosophy in matters of this sort was stated with startling and disconcerting simplicity. She was *willing to sacrifice* her personal liberty to protect " enslaved women."

By 1906 — the last year of Susan B. Anthony's life — she could look back on many successes and satisfactions. Four states had granted woman suffrage; women were being received on equal terms with men in colleges, industry, business, and the professions. The old legal disabilities against married women were being wiped off the statute books, and marriage was now a social contract between two equal partners. She could see that the legal and social revolution which she had led for more than half a century had produced substantial results. It had helped to liberate man as well as woman. But the dream was unfulfilled; the constitutional amendment had eluded her.

In her last speech on her eighty-sixth birthday she said: " What I ask is not praise, but justice." She was accorded both. From the most ridiculed and maligned of women, she became the most honored and respected. There is historic justice in the greatest of her triumphs. One hundred years after her birth the Nineteenth Amendment, giving women the right to vote, was ratified.

9

Oliver Wendell Holmes

Felix Frankfurter

Felix Frankfurter has been Associate Justice of the United States Supreme Court since 1939. He taught law at Harvard Law School from 1914 to 1939, after serving as assistant United States Attorney and as law officer in the Bureau of Insular Affairs. His books include *The Case of Sacco and Vanzetti, The Business of the Supreme Court, The Labor Injunction, Public and Its Government,* and *Mr. Justice Holmes and the Supreme Court.* His papers and addresses have been published under the title of *Of Law and Men,* edited by P. Elman.

Oliver Wendell Holmes

Felix Frankfurter

Mr. Justice Holmes was born on March 8, 1841, and died on March 6, 1935. He thus lived within two days of ninety-four years. It is somewhat difficult to try to expound briefly the significance of this great man's long and active life. Necessarily, therefore, his achievements and their abiding importance will have to be conveyed inadequately, though, let us hope, with fair balance and in proper perspective.

Holmes was rooted in the Puritan tradition, and his personal attachment to its meaning and environment went deep. "I love every brick and shingle of the old Massachusetts towns where once they worked and prayed," he said of his Puritan ancestors in one of his frequent references to them. After leaving Boston, he regularly returned to its nearby North Shore to enjoy each year its dunes and rocks and barberry bushes with refreshing devotion. But even as a college student he was a Bostonian apart. Very early his curiosities far transcended his emotional attachments. From the time — before he was twenty — that he learned from Emerson the lesson of intellectual independence, his quest for understanding was hemmed in neither by geography nor by personal preferences. So whole-souled was his love of country that only fools could misunderstand when he said, "I do not pin my dreams for the future to my country or even to my race. . . . I think it not improbable that man, like the grub that prepares a chamber for the winged thing it never has seen but is to be — that man may have cosmic destinies that he does not understand." New Englander of New Englanders in his feelings all his life, Holmes disciplined himself against any kind of parochialism in his thinking. Because he so completely rid himself of it, he is a significant figure in the history of civilization and not merely a commanding American figure.

As a truth-seeking Puritan, then, he entered Harvard in the fall of 1857. But before he was graduated came the Civil War and Lincoln's call for men. In April, 1861, Holmes, just turned twenty, enlisted, and on September 4 he started south with his beloved regiment, the 20th Massachusetts, part of the Army of the Potomac, to share, except when disabled, in its notable history. Three times he was put out of action; his war experiences are the stuff of heroic tales.

On his return to Boston, invalided from the front, his personal distinction and his war record irresistibly combined to make of him a military hero. Bishop William Lawrence gives the contemporary picture: " I saw him, a young officer, marching off to the front. . . . I watched his record, for we boys were alert to the heroes of those days, and as he was brought back wounded again and again . . . he was seen on the streets of Boston, a handsome invalid, to the great delectation of the girls of the city. He was a romantic hero, built for it." He himself harbored no romantic notions about war. He saw too much of it. Indeed, he shocked patriotic sentimentalists by speaking of war as an " organized bore," just as later he was to offend those whom he regarded as social sentimentalists by his insistence that war is merely a phase of that permanent struggle which is the law of life.

War, when you are at it, is horrible and dull. It is only when time has passed that you see that its message was divine. I hope it may be long before we are called again to sit at that master's feet. But some teacher of the kind we all need. In this smug, over-safe corner of the world we need it, that we may realize that our comfortable routine is no eternal necessity of things, but merely a little space of calm in the midst of the tempestuous untamed streaming of the world, and in order that we may be ready for danger. We need it in this time of individualist negations, with its literature of French and American humor, revolting at discipline, loving fleshpots, and denying that anything is worthy of reverence, — in order that we may remember all that buffoons forget. We need it everywhere and at all times.

These were the convictions he took out of the Civil War. These were the ideas that dominated him for the long years to come, for the Civil War probably cut into him more deeply than any other influence in his life. If it did not generate, it certainly fixed his conception of man's destiny. "I care not very much for the form if in some way he has learned that he cannot set himself over against the universe as a rival god, to criticize it, or to shake his fist at the skies, but that his meaning is its meaning, his only worth is as a part of it, as a humble instrument of the universal power."

This faith he expressed as a returning soldier and he repeated it, in enduring phrases endlessly varied, for seventy years in talk, in letters, in speeches, in opinions. But his "Soldier's Faith" was not merely an eloquent avowal of his philosophic beliefs regarding man's destiny, nor was it a gifted man's expression, in emotionally charged phrases, of what seemed to him "the key to intellectual salvation" as well as "the key to happiness." Holmes lived his faith. It would be difficult to conceive a life more self-conscious of its directions and more loyal in action to the faith which it espoused. His faith determined the very few personal choices he was called upon to make after he left the army; it was translated into concreteness in the multifarious cases that came before him for judgment for half a century.

He left the army because his term was up. In later life he said that if he had to do it again he would have stayed through the war. Instead, in the fall of 1864, he began the study of law. On graduating from Harvard Law School in 1866, he made the first of his numerous visits to England.

England had a strong pull for Holmes. "I value everything that shows the quiet unmelodramatic power to stand and take it in your people," wrote Holmes to Sir Frederick Pollock early in

World War I. But he could be sharp in detecting any tendency toward condescension or insensitiveness. He was a proud American who had no sympathy with suggestions of inadequacy of the American environment for finer sensibilities.

After his visit to England, Holmes settled down to the serious business of law. He entered it with strong misgivings and not for years were they quieted. The magnetic disturbance was philosophy. But in 1886, to students whom his old anxieties might beset, he was able to say " no longer with any doubt — that a man may live greatly in the law as elsewhere; that there as well as elsewhere his thought may find its unity in an infinite perspective; that there as well as elsewhere he may wreak himself upon life, may drink the bitter cup of heroism, may wear his heart out after the unattainable."

In 1867 he was admitted to the bar and began to practice his profession. With fierce assiduity he set himself to become master of his calling. " I should think Wendell worked too hard," wrote William James in 1869, and the theme recurs in the correspondence of the James family. Holmes never made a fetish of long hours, however; indeed, he believed that what he called work — really creative labor — could not be pursued for more than four hours a day. But he worked with almost feverish intensity. Holmes soaked himself in the details of the law. When he began, " the law presented itself as a ragbag of details. . . . it was not without anguish that one asked oneself whether the subject was worthy of the interest of an intelligent man." But his imaginative and philosophic faculties imparted life and meaning to dry details. Where others found only unrelated instances he saw vital connection. Thus it was true of him, as he said of another, that his knowledge " was converted into the organic tissue of wisdom."

During all these years he was in active practice, getting desirable glimpses into actualities. But his temperament being what it was, scholarly pursuits, though a sideline, doubtless enlisted his deepest interests. He would have welcomed appointment to the

United States District Court for the greater intellectual freedom it would have afforded him. But destiny had other plans for him.

The early writings of Holmes canvassed issues which are vital to a society devoted to justice according to law. What are the sources of law and what are its sanctions? What is appropriate lawmaking by courts and what should be left to legislation? What are the ingredients, conscious or unconscious, of adjudication? What are the wise demands of precedent and when should the judicial process feel unbound by its past? Such were the inquiries that guided Holmes's investigations at a time when law was generally treated as a body of settled doctrines from which answers to the new problems of a rapidly industrialized society were to be derived by a process of logical deduction. But in rejecting a view of law which regarded it as a merely logical unfolding Holmes had nothing in common with later tendencies toward a retreat from reason. By disproving formal logic as the revealer of social wisdom he did not embrace antirationalism. Quite the contrary. His faith was in reason and in motives not confined to material or instinctive desires. He refused to believe the theory that " the Constitution primarily represents the triumph of the money power over democratic agrarianism & individualism. . . . I shall believe until compelled to think otherwise that they [the leaders in establishing the Union] wanted to make a nation and invested (bet) on the belief that they would make one, not that they wanted a powerful government because they had invested. Belittling arguments always have a force of their own, but you and I believe that high-mindedness is not impossible to man." Equally so, while fully aware of the clash of interests in society and of law's mediating function, Holmes had nothing in common with the crude notion according to which law is merely the verbalization of prevailing force and appetites.

But at a time when judges boasted a want of philosophy, Holmes realized that decisions are functions of some juristic philosophy, and that awareness of the considerations that move beneath the surface of logical form is the prime requisite of a civilized system of law. In his analysis of judicial psychology, he was conscious of the role of the unconscious more than a generation before Freud began to influence modern psychology.

In 1881, before he was forty, he published *The Common Law*. The book marks an epoch for law and learning. Together with half a dozen of his essays, *The Common Law* gave the most powerful direction to legal science. He reoriented legal inquiry. The book is a classic in the sense that its stock of ideas has been absorbed and become part of common juristic thought. A few of its opening sentences give its drift. They represent the thought of today more truly than the temper of the time in which they were written. More than sixty years ago they placed law in a perspective which legal scholarship ever since has merely confirmed.

The life of the law has not been logic: it has been experience. The felt necessities of the time, the prevalent moral and political theories, intuitions of public policy, avowed or unconscious, even the prejudices which judges share with their fellow-men, have had a good deal more to do than the syllogism in determining the rules by which men should be governed. The law embodies the story of a nation's development through many centuries, and it cannot be dealt with as if it contained only the axioms and corollaries of a book of mathematics. In order to know what it is, we must know what it has been, and what it tends to become. We must alternately consult history and existing theories of legislation. But the most difficult labor will be to understand the combination of the two into new products at every stage. The substance of the law at any given time pretty nearly corresponds, so far as it goes, with what is then understood to be convenient; but its form and machinery, and the degree to which it is able to work out desired results, depend very much upon its past.

A work of such seminal scholarship as *The Common Law* makes its way only slowly in affecting the mode of thought of practitioners and judges; but it achieved prompt recognition from the learned world. Its immediate result was a call to Holmes from the Harvard Law School. But he soon exchanged the chair for the bench. On January 3, 1883, Holmes took his seat on the highest court of Massachusetts and for close to half a century he remained a judge.

The stream of litigation that flowed through such an important tribunal as the Supreme Judicial Court of Massachusetts during the twenty years of his incumbency enabled Holmes to fertilize the whole vast field of law. Although questions came before him in the unpremeditated order of litigation, his Massachusetts opinions — nearly thirteen hundred, scattered in fifty forbidding volumes — would, if appropriately brought together, constitute the most comprehensive and philosophic body of American law for any period of its history. For him they had the painful inadequacy of one whose aim was the unattainable.

I look into my book in which I keep a docket of the decisions of the full court which fall to me to write, and find about a thousand cases. A thousand cases, many of them upon trifling or transitory matters, to represent nearly half a lifetime! A thousand cases, when one would have liked to study to the bottom and to say his say on every question which the law has ever presented, and then to go on and invent new problems which should be the test of doctrine, and then to generalize it all and write it in continuous, logical, philosophic exposition, setting forth the whole corpus with its roots in history and its justifications of expedience real or supposed!

Such standards were doubtless stimulating to a bar, but were hardly calculated to receive universal approval. We have a trustworthy view of him as he appeared to lawyers who came before him in Massachusetts:

Nobody who sat on this Court in my time had quite such a daunting personality, — to a young lawyer at least. He was entirely courteous, but his mind was so extraordinarily quick and incisive, he was such an alert and sharply attentive listener, his questions went so to the root of the case, that it was rather an ordeal to appear before him. In arguing a case you felt that when your sentence was half done he had seen the end of it, and before the argument was a third finished that he had seen the whole course of reasoning and was wondering whether it was sound.

He hated long-windedness and recommended to the gentlemen of the bar the reading of French novels to cultivate the art of innuendo. He expressed himself, however, with sufficient explicitness in some labor cases to be deemed " dangerous " in important circles in Boston. Such was the direction of his thought at the time that a dissenting opinion which has since established itself as a great landmark in legal analysis on both sides of the Atlantic was seriously felt to be an obstacle to his judicial promotion. He had simply adhered to his detached view of the law and refused to translate fear of " socialism " " into doctrines that had no proper place in the Constitution or the common law."

He became Chief Justice of Massachusetts on August 5, 1899; and the very opinions which disturbed the conservatism of Boston were in part the influences that led President Theodore Roosevelt to look in Holmes's direction when a vacancy occurred on the Supreme Bench.

Holmes took his seat on December 8, 1902. He came to the Court at a time when vigorous legislative activity reflected changing social conceptions, which in turn were stimulated by vast technological development. What was in the air has been well epitomized by the observation that Theodore Roosevelt " was the first President of the United States who openly proposed to use the powers of political government for the purpose of affecting the distribution of wealth in the interest of the golden mean."

Though formally the product of ordinary lawsuits, constitutional law differs profoundly from ordinary law. Constitutional law is the body of doctrines by which the Supreme Court marks the boundaries between national and state action and by means of which it mediates between citizen and government. The Court thus exercises functions that determine vital arrangements in the government of the American people. The adjustments are

based, for the most part, on very broad provisions of the Constitution. Words like " liberty " and phrases like " due process of
law " and " regulate Commerce . . . among the several States,"
furnish the text for the judgment upon the validity of governmental action directed toward the infinite variety of social and economic facts. But these are words and phrases of " convenient
vagueness." They unavoidably give wide judicial latitude in determining the undefined and ever-shifting boundaries between
State and Nation, between freedom and authority. In a federated nation, especially one as vast in its territory and varied in its
interests as the United States, the power must be somewhere to
make the necessary accommodation between the central government and the states. The agency, moreover, must be one not subject to the vicissitudes and pressures under which the political
branches of government rest. The Supreme Court is that ultimate arbiter.

Holmes's profound analysis of the sources of our law before he
became a judge left in him an abiding awareness of the limited
validity of legal principles. He never forgot that circumstances
had shaped the law in the past, and that the shaping of future law
is primarily the business of legislatures. He was therefore keenly
sensitive to the subtle forces that are involved in the process of
reviewing the judgment of others not as to its wisdom but as to
its reasonableness of their belief in its wisdom. As society became
more and more complicated and individual experience correspond-
ingly narrower, tolerance and humility in passing judgment on
the experience and beliefs of legislators emerge as the decisive
factors in constitutional adjudication. No judge could be more
aware than was Holmes of these subtle aspects of the business of
deciding constitutional cases. He read omnivorously to " multi-
ply my scepticisms." His imagination and humility, rigorously
cultivated, enabled him to transcend the narrowness of his immediate experience. Probably no man who ever sat on the Court
was by temperament and discipline freer from emotional com-

mitments compelling him to translate his own economic or social views into constitutional commands. He did not read merely his own mind to discover the powers that may be exercised by a great nation. His personal views often ran counter to legislation which came before him for judgment. He privately distrusted attempts at improving society by what he deemed futile if not mischievous economic tinkering. But that was not his business. It was not for him to prescribe for society or to deny it the right of experimentation within very wide limits. That was to be left for contest by the political forces in the state. The duty of the Court was to keep the ring free. He reached the democratic result by the philosophic route of skepticism — by his disbelief in ultimate answers to social questions. Thereby he exhibited the judicial function at its purest.

He gave such ample scope to legislative judgment on economic policy because he knew so well to what great extent social arrangements are conditioned by time and circumstances. He also knew that we have " few scientifically certain criteria of legislation, and as it often is difficult to mark the line where what is called the police power of the States is limited by the Constitution of the United States, judges should be slow to read into the latter a *nolumus mutare* as against the law-making power." But social development is an effective process of trial and error only if there is the fullest possible opportunity for the free play of the mind. He therefore attributed very different legal significance to those liberties which history has attested as the indispensable conditions of a free society from that which he attached to liberties which derived merely from shifting economic arrangements. Even freedom of speech, however, he did not erect into a dogma of absolute validity nor did he enforce it to doctrinaire limits.

For him the Constitution was not a literary document but an instrument of government. As such it was to be regarded not as an occasion for juggling with words but as a means for ordering the life of a people. It had its roots in the past — " historic continuity with the past," he reminded his hearers, " is not a duty, it is only a necessity " — but it was also designed for the unknown future. This conception of the Constitution was the background against which he projected every inquiry into the scope of a specific power or specific limitation. That the Constitution is a framework of great governmental powers to be exercised for great public ends was for him not a pale intellectual concept. It dominated his process of constitutional adjudication. His opinions, composed in harmony with his dominating attitude toward the Constitution, recognized an organism within which the dynamic life of a free society can unfold and flourish. From his constitutional opinions there emerges the conception of a Nation adequate to its national and international tasks, whose federated States, though subordinate to central authority for national purposes, have ample power for their diverse local needs. He was mindful of the Union which he helped to preserve at Ball's Bluff, Antietam, and Fredericksburg. He was equally alert to assure scope for the States in matters peculiarly theirs because not within the reach of Congress.

With his vast learning he combined extraordinary rapidity of decision. His opinions were felicitous distillates of these faculties. His genius — put to service by rigorous self-discipline and deep learning — was to go for the essentials and express them with stinging brevity. He was impatient with laboring the obvious as a form of looseness, for looseness and stuffiness equally bored him. He genially suggested that judges need not be heavy to be weighty: ". . . our reports were dull because we had the notion that judicial dignity required solemn fluffy speech, as, when I grew up, everybody wore black frock coats, and black cravats. . . ."

In his opinions the thinker and the artist are superbly fused. In deciding cases, his aim was " to try to strike the jugular." His opinions appear effortless — birds of brilliant plumage pulled from the magician's sleeves. But his correspondence gives glimpses of the great effort that lay behind the seemingly easy achievement. "Of course in letters one simply lets oneself go without thinking of form but in my legal writing I do try to make it decent and I have come fully to agree with Flaubert. He speaks of writing French, but to write any language is enormously hard. To avoid vulgar errors and pitfalls ahead is a job. To arrange the thoughts so that one springs naturally from that which precedes it and to express them with a singing variety is the devil and all." And again: "The eternal effort of art, even the art of writing legal decisions, is to omit all but the essentials."

On the Supreme Court of the United States the expression of dissenting views on constitutional issues has, from the beginning, been deemed almost obligatory. In Washington, therefore, they came from Justice Holmes's pen more frequently than they had in Massachusetts, and sometimes were written with "cold Puritan passion." Some of his weightiest utterances are dissents, but they are dissents that have shaped history. Disproportionate significance has been attached to his dissents, however; they are merely a part of a much larger, organic whole.

After his retirement he played briefly with the suggestion that he put his ultimate thoughts on law between the covers of a small book, but all his life he had been driven by the lash of some duty undone and at last he revelled in the joy of having no unfinished business. Moreover, he felt strongly that he had had his say in the way in which he most cared to express his reflections — scattered in his more than two thousand opinions and in his lean but weighty collection of occasional writings. "I am being happily idle," he wrote to Pollock, "and persuading myself that 91 has outlived duty. . . ." He was no believer in systems. These, he felt, were heavy elaborations of a few insights — *aperçus*, to use his recurring word. Systems die; insights remain, he reiterated. Therefore, a few of his own *aperçus* will give the best clues to his philosophy of law and to his judicial technique in the most important field of his labors.

. . . the provisions of the Constitution are not mathematical formulas having their essence in their form; they are organic living institutions transplanted from English soil. Their significance is vital not formal; it is to be gathered not simply by taking the words and a dictionary, but by considering their origin and the line of their growth.

. . . when we are dealing with words that also are a constituent act, like the Constitution of the United States, we must realize that they have called into life a being the development of which could not have been foreseen completely by the most gifted of its begetters. It was enough for them to realize or to hope that they had created an organism; it has taken a century and has cost their successors much sweat and blood to prove that they created a nation. The case before us must be considered in the light of our whole experience and not merely in that of what was said a hundred years ago.

Great constitutional provisions must be administered with caution. Some play must be allowed for the joints of the machine, and it must be remembered that legislatures are ultimate guardians of the liberties and welfare of the people in quite as great a degree as the courts.

It is futile to try to account for genius; and the term is not inaptly used for one whom so qualified an appraiser as Mr. Justice Cardozo deemed probably the greatest legal intellect in the history of the English-speaking judiciary. Holmes simply heeded his own deepest impulses. He was born to probe beyond the surface of things, to cut beneath the skin of formulas, however respectable. He looked beneath their decorous formulations and saw them for what they usually are — sententious expressions of overlapping or conflicting social policies. The vital judicial issue is apt, therefore, to be their accommodation. Decisions thus become essentially a matter of drawing lines. Again and again he adverted to that necessity, which he once summed up as follows: "I do not think we need trouble ourselves with the thought that my view depends upon differences of degree. The whole law does so as soon as it is civilized. . . ." Such a view of law of course implies the exercise of choice. But judicial judgment precluded the notion of capricious choice. It assumes judgment between defined claims, each of recognized validity and with a cultural pedigree of its own, but all of which necessarily cannot be completely satisfied. This process of adjustment is bound increasingly to fall to the legislature as interests and activities in society become more and more interdependent. The considerations which thus prompt legislation and the intricate, dubious materials out of which laws are written bring into sharp focus the duty of deference to legislative determinations demanded from the revisory process called adjudicative. In a thousand instances Holmes was loyal to that philosophy. Thereby he resolved into comprehending larger truths the conflicting claims of State and Nation, of liberty and authority, of individual and society.

"It is right and proper that in the reading room of the Harvard Law School the portrait of Holmes should face in equal honor the portrait of Marshall." There fell to Marshall, as Holmes took occasion to say, "perhaps the greatest place that ever was filled by a judge." That Marshall seized it, the role of the Supreme Court in American history bears witness. Holmes's claim to preeminence has a different basis. He is unsurpassed in the depth of his penetration into the nature of the judicial process and in the originality of its exposition. His conception of the Constitution cannot be severed from his conception of a judge's function in applying it; and his views of the judge's function derive from his intellectual presuppositions, that is, from his loyal adherence in judicial practice to his philosophic skepticism. His approach to judicial problems was inseparable from his consciously wrought notions of his relations to the universe. These abstractions appear far removed from the particular cases that came before him. But the clarity with which a specific controversy is seen, in the context of the larger intellectual issues beneath the formal surface of litigation, and the disinterestedness with which such analysis guides decision and opinion are the ultimate determinants of American public law.

After a major operation in the summer of 1922, Holmes showed signs of age — he was then in his eighty-second year — but his mar-

velous physique gradually reasserted itself, though he strictly con-
served his energy for his work. Some of his most powerful opinions were written in his ninth decade. Until near the end of his
tenure he usually wrote more than his share of opinions. He was
nearly eighty-nine when the illness and death of Chief Justice
Taft cast upon Holmes for a considerable period the heavy burden of presiding in Court and the still more difficult task of guiding its deliberations at conferences. He did both, in the language
of Mr. Justice Brandeis, " as to the manner born."

The machinery was running down, however, and on January
12, 1932, he sent his resignation to the President — " the time has
come and I bow to the inevitable." He continued his serene life,
in Washington and in the summers at Beverly Farms, reading and
being read to, enjoying the simple and familiar things of nature
that had always refreshed him and the devoted attention of
friends, especially the young. He had become a very old man but
his faculties were never impaired. He had grown almost wistful
in his gentleness. The fire of his exciting personality was dying
down and on the morning of March 6, 1935, came the end.

With the sure response of the mass of men — given enough time
— to goodness and gallantry of spirit, Holmes, the fundamentally
solitary thinker, had become a pervasive and intimate national possession. His death elicited an outpouring of feeling throughout
the country. But of all the moving things that were said, he
would probably have most liked the few words of his old friend
and his closest colleague for fifteen years, Mr. Justice Brandeis,
when the news was brought to him: " And so the great man is
gone." On his ninety-fourth birthday — a raw March day with
snow gently falling — he was buried with due military honors in
the Arlington National Cemetery, alongside his wife and near his
companions, known and unknown, of the Army of the Potomac.

Without accompanying explanation, he left the bulk of his substantial estate to the Nation, the largest unrestricted gift ever
made to it. Congress established a Holmes Fund Memorial Com-

mission. In a message to that body recommending an appropriate use of the bequest, President Franklin Roosevelt thus interpreted Holmes's intention: "It is the gift of one who, in war and in peace, devoted his life to its [his country's] service. Clearly he thereby sought, with a generous emphasis, to mark the full measure of his faith in those principles of freedom which the country was founded to preserve." And the President expressed what he deemed to be the country's desire that Congress "translate this gift into a form that may serve as a permanent impulse for the maintenance of the deepest tradition that Mr. Justice Holmes embodied." That tradition, wrote President Roosevelt, "was a faith in the creative possibilities of the law. For him law was an instrument of just relations between man and man. With an insight into its history that no American scholar has surpassed; with a capacity to mold ancient principles to present needs, unique in range and remarkable in prophetic power; with a grasp of its significance as the basis upon which the purposes of men are shaped, Mr. Justice Holmes sought to make the jurisprudence of the United States fulfill the great ends our nation was established to accomplish."

10

Woodrow Wilson

Samuel Steinberg

Samuel Steinberg, chairman of the Social Studies Department at Stuyvesant High School, New York City, has also taught in the extension divisions of Brooklyn College and New York University. In 1947–48 he served as director of vocational rehabilitation in the United States Zone of Germany. He is the author of a number of textbooks in the fields of government and history, including *The United States: Story of a Free People.*

Woodrow Wilson

Samuel Steinberg

Few Presidents faced more hectic times than did Woodrow Wilson when he entered the White House on March 4, 1913. The old order seemed to be shaking everywhere. At home, workers and farmers and suffragettes were clamoring for sweeping reforms. While their demands were being pressed, foreign crises, including the specter of a world war, were intruding themselves. And no President understood better than Wilson did the characterization of the Presidency by a later historian: " He [the President] is, or can be, the essence of the nation's personality. In him many things can flower or decay." Woodrow Wilson, keen student of American politics, knew that the Presidency in times of crisis meant the double role of ruler and scapegoat. He had written:

The President cannot escape being the leader of his party, except by incapacity and lack of personal force, because he is at once the choice of the party and of the nation. . . . His is the only *national* voice in affairs. Let him once win the admiration and confidence of the country, and no other single force can withstand him, no combination of forces will easily overpower him. His position takes the imagination of the country. He is the representative of no constituency, but of the whole people. He may be both the leader of his party and the leader of the nation or he may be one or the other. If he leads the nation, his party can hardly resist him.

Woodrow Wilson had no fear of the Presidency in time of peace, for he knew his politics, and he had faith in his ability to handle men and controversial issues. But he dreaded war, not only because of its wanton destruction and utter uselessness, but also because he knew war distorts the straight lines of reason and makes difficult the tasks of sane and wise leadership. He was in particular fear of the impending European war. It was for this reason that he sent Colonel House, his personal adviser, on a peace mission to the courts of Europe in the spring of 1914. House reported to the White House, " The situation is extraordinary. It is militarism run stark mad. Unless someone acting for you can bring about a different understanding, there is some day to be an awful cataclysm. No one in Europe can do it. . . . It is an absorbing problem and one of tremendous consequences. I wish it might be solved to the everlasting glory of our American civilization." Unfortunately, the negotiations were stultified by blind arrogance and utter lack of comprehension of consequences. The war came two months later.

" Why this dread fear of war? " one may ask. Was Wilson a timid, Buchanan-like personality, who shied away from conflict and struggle? Nothing can be further from the truth. With the fire and moral indignation of an ancient prophet, Woodrow Wilson was the kind of man who held firmly to a principle even if it involved turning a deaf ear to close and trusted advisers. But he knew that war impoverishes people materially and spiritually. At one time he remarked to his friend Irving Cobb, " Once lead the people into war and they will forget there was ever such a thing as tolerance. To fight, you must be brutal and ruthless. The spirit of ruthless brutality will enter the very fibre of our national life." This prophecy was tragically fulfilled in Wilson himself, when, during the war, he had Congress enact Constitution-crippling espionage and anti-free speech laws. Even conservatives like Charles Evans Hughes, onetime Chief Justice, shuddered at what war did to the apostle of the New Freedom. Whether it was the war that damaged Wilson or whether it was a growing illness is still a moot point. At any rate, his attitude toward civil liberties must be viewed as one of the ironies of history.

No wonder, then, that when the false news telling of the election of Charles Evans Hughes came (the California results were four days late in 1916), Wilson exclaimed "Thank God!" He felt relieved that a second term would not be his. He felt relieved because he knew the clouds of American involvement in the war were on the horizon. And so it was with a heavy heart that Woodrow Wilson, who by training and temperament was geared to a life of constructive peace, faced his second administration. In spite of all efforts at neutrality during his first administration, this man of peace was destined to become a war President of the first magnitude. His very belief in the might of right, as against the right of might, prompted him to stir up the American people against the German military machine that was then threatening the civilized world.

Wilson was happiest during his first term, for it was then that he was able to lead his country that he loved so well to a deeper conception of democracy. Like Andrew Jackson and Abraham Lincoln, he had a passionate faith in the common people. This faith is well expressed in his First Inaugural Address:

We have been proud of our industrial achievements but we have not hitherto stopped thoughtfully enough to count the human cost. . . . Our thought has been "Let every man look out for himself, let every generation look out for itself," while we reared giant machinery which made it impossible that any but those who stood at the levers of control should have a chance to look out for themselves. . . . The great Government we loved has often been made use of for private and selfish purposes and those who use it had forgotten the people. . . . There can be no equality or opportunity . . . if men, and women, and children be not shielded in their lives, their very vitality, from the consequences of great industrial and social processes which they cannot alter, control or singly cope with. Society must see to it that it does not itself crush or weaken, or damage its own constituent parts.

In this clear pronouncement, Wilson added a new dimension to democracy. He departed from the Jeffersonian principle of the less government the better, which had been attuned to a nineteenth-century rural society. He heralded a new principle for

the young century — specifically, that if the individual is to sur-
vive in a complex industrial society, the government must use its
influence and power to contain the strong so that the weak may
enjoy a reasonable amount of opportunity. Wilson's liberalism
thus departed from the historical, classical liberalism that had
been wedded to laissez-faire economics. Rather, it is identical
with the reform movement that has aimed to conciliate economic
and political freedom with the general welfare. To achieve these
ends, Wilson determined to carry forward Teddy Roosevelt's
conviction that an executive must exert all the leadership of which
he is capable.

How was this determination to be translated into national policy? Certainly not by viewing the Presidency as the supine agent
of Congress, nor by viewing the executive branch as a mere check
of the legislature, nor by forfeiting the leadership of his party to
bosses and demagogues. The President once commented, "no
party can for any length of time control the government or serve
the people, which cannot command the allegiance of its own minority." As early as the 1890's, when Wilson was professor of
political science at Princeton, he sensed the growing importance
of the administrative arm of the government. In a famous essay,
"The Study of Administration," he wrote at that time these prophetic words, "Like a lusty child, government with us has expanded in nature and grown great in stature, but has also become
awkward in movement. The vigor and increase of its life has
been altogether out of proportion to its skill in living. It has
gained strength but it has not acquired deportment." On another
occasion, Wilson pointed out that the Constitution "was not
meant to hold the government back to the time of horses and
wagons, the time when postboys carried every communication."

In other words, a quarter of a century before he became President, Wilson saw the importance of streamlining and adding
power to the executive branch. He knew, too, that the force of
historical events was constantly creating situations for which the

Constitution proved an inadequate guide and that it was important for Presidents to create precedents on which their successors could draw. But it is one thing to know that something has to be done and it is another to be able to do it. How was Wilson going to put across his ideas of the New Democracy and his ideas of Big Government, so essential to keep in check the dynamic march of Big Business? For this the President had to possess the vision of the statesman and the skill of the master politician.

These qualities Wilson had to a remarkable degree. Never a speculative thinker, this " scholar in politics " was always eager to put ideas into practical use. If the businessman were to dare to start a panic to thwart Wilson's reform measures, " I promise him [the businessman]," warned the President, " not for myself, but for my countrymen, a gibbet as high as Haman." By fusing the varied demands for domestic reform with the national yearning for peace, Wilson, a minority President (he received less than 42 per cent of the popular vote in the election of 1912), succeeded in getting himself accepted as a symbol of national unity.

Accordingly, under the inspiration of the President's leadership, Congress passed a series of laws which Wilson himself later referred to as the New Freedom. A strong believer in the ultimate wisdom of international trade, the President appeared before Congress in person (a practice abandoned since the days of John Adams), and persuaded the Legislature to make sharp reductions in the tariff. A consistent, forthright, and clear champion of the little man, he successfully urged Congress to include a provision in the tariff law for a graduated income tax based upon the principle, " from each according to his ability to pay." Thus this first income tax under the Sixteenth Amendment got off to what Wilson thought was a truly democratic implementation. Alarmed by Wall Street's control of the nation's credit facilities and by the inadequacies of the banking system as revealed by the panic of 1907, Congress, under the President's leadership, set up the Federal Reserve System, thereby dispersing the concentrated power of the banking interests into twelve federal branches. Mindful of the dangers of monopolies to our competitive system and to the public at large, Wilson had Congress put on the statute books a powerful antitrust law which aimed to re-establish " effective competition." Sensitive to Samuel Gompers' plea that organized labor should not be outlawed, Wilson had Congress write into this same antitrust law a provision which strengthened the position of trade unions by making them immune to prosecution as trusts. True to the traditions of the United States as an asylum for the oppressed of the world, he twice vetoed, although in vain, the Literacy Act, which he thought discriminated against Eastern and Southern European immigrants and which would close the door to those seeking the " opportunity of education." Risking unpopularity in certain quarters and believing unflinchingly in merit, Wilson appointed Louis Brandeis, " Champion of social justice," to the Supreme Court of the United States — an appointment that was hailed by progressives as an important milestone in the history of the Republic. Turning its back on the tradition of " no federal aid to the schools of the nation; education is the sole responsibility of the state," the New Freedom launched two basic laws that offered to the states federal aid for vocational training programs on the college and high school level. Thus the principle of federal aid to education without federal control was established.

Did the New Freedom show Wilson to be a wild-eyed radical, a promoter of socialism? Shortsighted, selfish men thought so. But many of those citizens who had at heart the general welfare and those citizens who had enough vision to understand what was good for the future security of their country supported the President. Wilson's supporters hailed him as a great liberal who was simply carrying on from where Jackson and Lincoln and Teddy Roosevelt had left off. The future proved them to be right. For example, is there today any responsible person, no matter how conservative, who would advocate the destruction of the Federal Reserve System? Yet, in Wilson's days, this capstone of the New Freedom was viewed as the very invention of a socialist devil. "Preposterous offspring of ignorance and unreason," said the opponents of the Federal Reserve System. A glance at the other great reforms of the New Freedom will reveal that they, too, have become invaluable to American democracy.

Seen from the perspective of history, we now judge Wilson to have been a liberal, not an ideologist or doctrinaire. If he attacked the entrenched prerogatives and powers, he was not expressing the interest of a single social class in contradistinction, but he was articulating the voices of the majority of the American people, who had been grumbling ever since the Progressive Era got under way. The legislation Wilson sponsored did not spring from preconceived assumptions that the interests of the different classes were wholly contradictory. The New Freedom was engineered in the name of the democratic principle that economic groups *can* be conciliated. This truly liberal position thus rejects the Marxian doctrine that sets up a perpetual dichotomy between social classes. This liberal position thus refuses to set as its goal the total annihilation or suppression of the competing group or groups. In short, the New Freedom conformed in a real sense with the experimental and pragmatic tenets that have up to now proved to be the genius of the American people.

A flash back to his pre-presidential career reveals another aspect of Wilson's heart and mind. Like Jefferson, he recognized very clearly the connection between the responsibility of leadership and education. With Jefferson, he believed that no people could properly expect to be free and ignorant. This interest is seen clearly throughout Wilson's career as professor and, later, as president of Princeton. "The business of the world," he declared, "is not individual success but its own betterment, its own strengthening, and its own growth in spiritual insight." Universities, he felt, were not country clubs for "gentlemen loafers," but experimental laboratories where independent-minded professors and diligent students experienced the fine arts of free inquiry and democratic living. Thus did Wilson, the first non-clerical president of Princeton, achieve a reputation as educational leader second only to Charles W. Eliot of Harvard.

Wilson's university work against the background of the general reform movement won for him the popularity that brought him to the governorship of the state of New Jersey. Although his career as governor was confined to a single term (1911–1913), he established enough of a reform record, in spite of the machine politicians, to attract the attention of the nation. When he won the Democratic nomination in 1912 over his opponent, Speaker Champ Clark of Missouri, it was as a reform governor whose leadership had succeeded in enacting the " seven sisters " laws for ending the notoriously lax corporation laws of New Jersey.

Had Woodrow Wilson failed to be re-elected in 1916, he would have gone down in history as a great President on the record of his New Freedom. His second term made him a world renowned figure. The story of how America launched a preparedness program and then entered the war at a time when a member of the American Peace Society was in the White House is known to every schoolboy. But not enough is known about the tragedy that befell the American people and the people of the world when the foreign policy of the great President was abandoned.

Wilson, long before we entered the war, made clear the foundations of his international policy. He simply applied to international politics the principle so nobly set forth by our Declaration of Independence — that no government was just that did not have the consent of the governed. We see this policy in his recognition of the Republic of Sun Yat Sen in China and in his determination not to recognize the dictatorship of Huerta in Mexico. We see it later on in his heartbreaking but necessary decision to ask Congress to declare war when it became clear that the Kaiser's war machine was torpedoing our policy of neutrality. Wilson had for a long time thought of resigning from the presidency — such was his aversion to war. He wondered why people cheered him as he drove along Pennsylvania Avenue after delivering the war message. "How strange to applaud a war message," he remarked to a friend. But the "war message" was really delivered by a mad German Empire bent on world conquest. Intervention came only after thirty-two months of anguished diplomacy marked by heroic efforts to prevent the outbreak of the war. When the Germans ordered the resumption of unrestricted submarine warfare there was only one thing left to do for the man who was "too proud to fight."

But Wilson, in his idealism, saw no excuse for war if it was merely to stop aggression. If the peace that followed meant only a cessation of military force and violence, it was bound to be merely a negative peace — a truce between wars. Such a peace meant the vain sacrifice of millions of young men. With zeal and determination, he therefore decided to make this war an end to all wars. It could have no other excuse. In keeping with this profound faith, Wilson launched his Fourteen Points. Briefly, these were to be: freedom of the seas for all nations; removal of economic barriers; reduction of armaments to the lowest point consistent with a nation's safety or security; settlement of colonial problems paying special attention to the needs of the colonial peoples; self-determination of small nationalities; and, finally, a League of Nations which would aim to make war forever a thing of the past. In short, the peace was to be a peace without victory. Whatever gain would result from such a program would be a gain for all humanity, not for any single nation or group of nations. The horrible sacrifices of the World War would not be in vain.

What happened to this peace? Partisan politics in the United States, coupled with the President's overzealousness — an overzealousness that caused him to ignore the imperatives of Realpolitik, which would have dictated congressional representation at the peace conference — spelled out the fateful round robin of March 2, 1919, whereby thirty-nine senators vowed opposition to the peace treaty of which the League of Nations was an integral part. In Europe, the " vengeful Clemenceau, the trimmer Orlando, the demagogic Lloyd George " hammered out a jingoistic peace that could mean only a prenatal death to the League. And too many citizens everywhere, stamping out the memories of their late sons, returned to a life of " business as usual." Even if the liberal forces both here and abroad might have effected a change, they were stymied by the fear of bolshevism that reared its head in the postwar world. Woodrow Wilson, alone in his vision, was put in a position of making compromise after compromise to save the League. Thus were sown the germs of World War II. Thus, according to Wilson, " a little group of willful men, representing no opinion but their own, have rendered the great government of the United States helpless and contemptible."

Wilson cried out in vain. " I can predict," said he, " with absolute certainty that within another generation there will be another world war if the world does not concert the method by which to prevent it." We know the tragic sequel. The second World War did come. Only this time, the people had acquired at great cost enough wisdom to give overwhelming support to the international body formed after this war.* Lest our support and enthusiasm for the United Nations do not diminish and in order to understand better the forces that have become antagonistic toward the United Nations it may be well for us to pause and analyze the real reasons that led to the rejection of the League of Nations.

Viewed in the perspective of almost two generations of history, the factor of Wilson's personality and leadership in the failure of

---

* Though we in the atomic age are closer to destruction than in 1914, we are better equipped, via collective security, to cope with lawlessness than was the international anarchy before 1914. To Wilson must be given credit for the dilution of the poisonous mixture called *Realpolitik* with the tincture of international morality.

the League must be construed as a negligible one. The basic factor of the American rejection of the League must be put at the door of the antiliberal forces that returned to power after 1920 and whose contempt for the New Freedom was transcendent. Hating Wilson's New Freedom, they determined to discredit all of Woodrow Wilson. Nothing he stood for must remain untarnished. The tunes of the Pied Pipers of Normalcy lured the war-tired population. Especially sweet were the tunes to the Gadarenes, who saw nothing but the immediate moment. It was these elements, in the minority, but powerful, which strengthened the irreconcilable isolationist senators. The latter were in a particularly good position to crack the whip because the League's commanding general had become desperately ill at a crucial time. And so the League died, as far as the United States was concerned; and without the United States, it was just a matter of a few years before the remnant would be no more.

On the occasion of the great President's death, on February 3, 1924, William Allen White, staunch but wise Republican, spoke these words of almost lyrical beauty. "God," said he, "gave Woodrow Wilson a great vision. . . . The proud heart is still. The vision lives." William Allen White uttered a prophetic truth. Wilson, in the realm of foreign politics, went down to defeat, but his vision lived on. He was defeated by the prejudices, the partialities, the selfishness and excitements of the moment. He spoke sense to his generation but he was defeated. However, from a larger viewpoint, Wilson triumphed. "Reason," said William James, "is one of the very feeblest of nature's forces, if you take it at any one spot and moment. It is only in the very long run that its effects become perceptible."

Woodrow Wilson's work, both as scholar and as statesman, represents an important step toward the realization of the American dream. The year 1912, the year of Wilson's election, saw a nation still under the heels of giant industrialists and financiers, who were unconsciously fomenting a social revolution. That same year also saw a world caught in a treacherous international anarchy without even a hope of airing its troubles before an international body, no matter how limited. The year 1921, when Woodrow Wilson departed from the White House, saw a nation well on the way to harnessing the monopolistic monster — not with mere trappings, but with the firm bridle of the New Freedom's laws. That same year also saw a world with a vision of an international order under which nations would some day learn to solve their disputes by instruments other than war. If there were economic collapses and world war still ahead, it would not be because Woodrow Wilson had failed.

Paraphrasing Sir Desmond MacCarthy's remarks about intellectuals, one may say that Woodrow Wilson was among those liberal statesmen who " like corals build the reef that protects the lagoon . . . from the restless sea of nonsense and confusion. Strong waves will burst against it, and some of them foam over. But the reef must be built." The nonsense and confusion of Normalcy followed the New Freedom. The strong waves of world depression and of world war burst upon the New Freedom and the League of Nations. But the reef survived to serve as a foundation of added bulwarks against man's follies. Whether these bulwarks stand against renewed nonsense and confusion depends upon the gods and, to a large extent, upon the American people. Whether our treasured civilization takes the place of a dinosaur in the catalogue of extinct species or whether it achieves new heights depends upon the restoration to *active* life everywhere of the sanity and justice so well preached by Woodrow Wilson.

II

John Dewey

Jerome Nathanson

Jerome Nathanson has served as an official of the National Child Labor Committee, the American Association of Arbitrators, the New York Society for Ethical Culture, and the International Humanist and Ethical Union. Author of *Forerunners of Freedom* and *John Dewey: The Reconstruction of the Democratic Life,* he is also the editor of *The Authoritarian Attempt to Capture Education* and *Science for Democracy.*

John Dewey

Jerome Nathanson

Probably more books about education are being published to-day than at any time in our history. A good portion of them are attacks on what used to be called " progressive " education or the " new " education. But while John Dewey was the intellectual and spiritual father of the whole movement, most of the critics are careful not to attack him. Instead, they continue to pay their respects to America's greatest philosopher, who died in 1952 at the age of ninety-two.

The influence of John Dewey on twentieth-century America is pervasive. Indeed, it is so much part of everything we are and do that it is difficult to distinguish it from the other influences which have shaped us. Certainly, for those of us born since 1900, Dewey is part of the very way we see things and think about them. We would indeed have been the poorer as persons if he had never done his work. There may be some who would dis-agree with this judgment. But poorer or not, we would have been somehow different, and that is the measure of his mark upon us.

Conversation, for most of us, is an affair of rapid exchange. One person says something and another immediately responds. Indeed, we frequently interrupt each other in our anxiety to say what we have to say. But a conversation with Dewey was alto-gether different. I recall the first opportunity I had of talking with him alone, with the words spilling out of me, and then the pause for Dewey's reply. The pause lengthened into a silence that became heavy with embarrassment — embarrassment that I had been making a fool of myself after all, embarrassment that Dewey had not even been listening, that his mind had somehow wandered. And finally, after what had seemed an eternity, came Dewey's reflections on what had been said, taking it all up into the retort of his mind, and giving back, not just a distillation, but something compounded of everything he was, brought to bear on this particular point.

This was the first time I had ever talked with a person who paid the subtle compliment of thinking protractedly about what I had said. Only, with Dewey, it was not a compliment but a matter of course; this was how he dealt with ideas. It is no wonder that Irwin Edman and many others have commented on this deliberate manner of his. For thousands of people Dewey was, and always will be, the living example of Emerson's " Man Thinking."

He thought of himself as first and foremost a philosopher, as he reminded us on the occasion of his ninetieth birthday. It is as a philosopher that Dewey will go down through the ages. Yet respect for ideas was, from one point of view, simply part of his respect for persons. It is common knowledge that he was always ready to do what he could for political and social causes in which he believed — and how he found time for all of them, no one will ever know. But, on the individual level, it seems that he was always available for anybody who wanted him for personal help.

There was the young poet, newly arrived in New York City, who had never met Dewey but was deeply anxious for the approval of one who had become a kind of idol to him. He spent days trying to track Dewey down and at last, locating the apartment, bundled a large batch of sonnets under his arm and went to call on the great man, without an appointment. Dewey asked him in and, interrupting whatever he was doing at the moment, then and there read over the sonnets and discussed them at some length.

Another young man who had just finished college and wanted to go on studying for his doctoral degree in education could not decide where he should go for his graduate work. Though he had never met Dewey, the young man sat down and wrote him in detail, outlining his problems and asking Dewey's advice. He was neither ignored nor dealt with perfunctorily. Instead, almost by return mail, he received Dewey's best thinking and best advice on the questions he had asked.

One is aware of a number of incidents of this kind. How many such persons must there be, not just in the United States but in all parts of the world, who were unknown to Dewey and yet turned to him because of what he was and what he symbolized for them, and were never turned away! It was with such experiences in mind that John Lovejoy Elliott, one of the great social workers and spiritual leaders of our time, once remarked: " I'm not sure I know where I come out on John Dewey's philosophy, but I know where I come out on John Dewey. The man's a saint, that's all! "

Whether or not he was a saint, he was surely the epitome of simplicity, as perhaps only a great human being can be. One picked up the telephone to talk with him and, until his last years, there was no secretary or other intermediary who answered for him. The phone would give a few rings and there would be the " Hello " in the familiar Yankee twang. One would go to his home and, after ringing the doorbell, would stand listening to the clack of the typewriter for a few moments, until Dewey himself opened the door. One would receive a letter from him in his unparalleled typescript, with the lines extending to the very edge of the page, ending at whatever point in a word they happened to end, with no hyphens; as if, trying to keep up with the pace of his thought, there just was not time enough to make it also look neat. One would see him come onto the lecture platform, looking somehow a little surprised if not abashed that so many people should come to hear him speak, though the flat drone of his voice frequently prevented his hearers from getting the eloquence of what he was saying.

But these, and other incidents like them, were only the paraphernalia, the tokens, of Dewey's simplicity. His real simplicity lay, as it must, in what he was. He was a man wholly and stubbornly committed to thinking what he had to think and saying what he had to say, never underestimating what he was trying to do, but never conceivably taking any personal credit for doing it.

This simplicity of his is not so manifest in his work, but it is there. For once one cuts beneath the tortuously careful and endlessly qualified language of his books, Dewey's ideas appear startlingly clear and simple. The ideas, essentially, are that nothing is more important to people than people; that no person or group of persons should ride herd over others; that the goods of life are such as to make a good life possible for everyone; that beauty is not a museum piece, not a dilettante's indulgence, but something that should characterize the common life; and that reason domesticated and put to human use as hardpan intelligence is our chief reliance in an uncertain but ever-promising world.

The ideas are simple and, perhaps because of that, they have world-shaking implications. For if we ever gave intelligence free play in behalf of a common humanity, who knows where it might lead. A free intelligence holds no institution sacred, not even private enterprise: that is why the National Association of Manufacturers distrusted Dewey. A free intelligence has no use for any dictatorship, not even the dictatorship of the proletariat: that is why the Communists hated Dewey. A free intelligence can never make its peace with dogmatism, not even when it wears the halo of religion: that is why the fundamentalist churches fought Dewey. Meanwhile, his ideas go on, in a way ideas have — not automatically but because, touching wellsprings of human need, they enlist human energies.

Ours is a day of obscurantism and hysteria, as Dewey frequently observed, in which men's anxieties have led many to believe that they can attain security only through the sacrifice of freedom. On all sides we are assured that science and secularism are at the root of contemporary evils and that somehow, through a mysterious method compatible with the mysteries it celebrates, we will find peace only by minimizing our knowledge. This is the meaning of obscurantism. Meanwhile, we are torn apart by a vague sense of guilt for the bestiality of this world, and project that guilt to those who challenge things as they are. This is the meaning of our hysteria. And increasingly, though knowing deep inside us that nothing is secure which cannot withstand attacks however virulent, we turn to authorities to stifle the dissenters among us. This is the meaning of our retreat from freedom.

The social, the institutional roots of this sickness of the modern world are there to be seen — if not by cursory examination, then by painstaking inquiry. But what is painstaking can also be painful, and there are those who find it easier and more comforting to " solve " problems through prophetic insight or intuition. This is sometimes dignified with the names of faith and revelation. The history of religious and philosophic thought is studded with the false problems stated and agonized over by those who took this course. Dewey was not among them. He saw philosophy, rather, as starting and ending with the problems of men. That is why, for all the difficulties of his style, he is always so down-to-earth. That is also why he has sometimes been called " the great destroyer."

Dewey well knew that the dominant tradition of western thought has centered around the idea that the universe is not all of a piece. On the contrary, according to this tradition, the world we know is mere surface or shadow, symbol or appearance. And, it is claimed, beneath or behind this world is reality. Religion, traditionally, has taken this to show that the meaning of life is not to be found in the here and now, but in some unseen world hereafter; and all that we experience is variously interpreted as a dream or a testing ground set up by a severe but loving Father. Philosophy has taken it to show that if we would know the " truth " we must rely upon reason or intuition or contemplation of what is unchanging and eternal.

From one point of view, this dualism — between appearance and reality, between the temporal and the eternal, between the uncertain and the certain — solves the basic human dilemma. It gives meaning to all the sweat and heartache of the world. It gives security to those who find it by having things pegged down once and for all. It gives substance to our aspirations and fulfillment to our dreams.

But Dewey was well aware of the problems to which this dualism has given rise, and how they have dogged mankind for centuries. If a loving Father is responsible for everything that is, how account for the cruelty and tragedy of life? If the world we know is not the real world, how can we ever "know" reality? These and similar questions, with all their endless and subtle ramifications, have absorbed the energies of countless men for countless years. And all the while, the problems of this world, of doing what we can with it and with ourselves, have persisted.

Supposing one assumes, however, that the universe is all of a piece, and that our experience is as real as anything else in it. Immediately the traditional problems change or disappear. If experience is not a counterfeit reality but the genuine article, then what happens to us here and now is of paramount importance. If whatever we know about experience is only probable and never certain, then we must recast our notions of what knowledge is, and develop ever better ways of knowing. If the things we value most in life — love, health, beauty, friendship, peace, freedom — are unstable and precarious, then our problem is not to find some mystical guarantee for them, but to make them as stable and persisting as we can.

Essentially, this is the assumption Dewey made, with all the consequences which follow from it. From the viewpoint of the great tradition, he pulled down the pillars of the temple. But he was not a mere destroyer. He was a rebuilder. And the reconstruction of our thinking and of our ways of living together, in order to give ever freer play to the best possibilities of men in democratic communities, is the burden of his work.

The educational revolution which Dewey spearheaded stems

from this. For traditionally, just as all life was regarded as a preparation for the hereafter, so schooling was seen as preparation of the child for adult or " real " life. The schools had their rituals no less than the churches, and training of the mind through a fixed curriculum — reading, writing, arithmetic — was thought to be the way to make children tractable if not civilized.

But once one sees experience as real, everything changes. Then life is not merely preparation, but life itself. Then a child's experience is not merely preparation, but important on its own account. Then schooling becomes a matter not simply of teaching children what adults think they ought to know, but of helping them to discover their own powers. Then training the mind, whatever that means, is seen as less vital than helping children to the richest possible experiences under intelligent guidance. Then instead of regarding children as little adults, we begin to study them for what they are, and we find that learning confined to verbal rote is a pale substitute for what one learns by doing things himself. This is the meaning of the famous slogan that we learn to do by doing. It is also the meaning of emphasis upon the child-centered school.

Because of this educational " revolution," there is hardly a teacher in America, or in the entire western world for that matter, who has not been influenced, either consciously or unconsciously, directly or indirectly, by Dewey's pedagogical thinking. That is a sobering consideration when we try to evaluate our school systems. The teachers have been influenced, and also the rest of us through the teachers. But what has been the nature of the influence, and its effectiveness?

We emphasize educating for democracy as the most important thing we have to do. But by and large we do not mean it. If we did, presumably the two generations already influenced by this teaching would now at least be willing to pay for proper schooling. Instead, at the same time that we emphasize more and better training for teachers, we put them in overcrowded schools with inadequate facilities, where they cannot possibly teach as they have been trained to do. We stress the idea that the school should be a democratic community, animated by a sense of common humanity and common purposes, but we permit teachers and pupils alike to be segregated along sectarian religious lines. And the simple faith in persons and intelligence, which is at the root of this philosophy, is everywhere on the defensive before the militant onslaughts of authoritarian-minded religious leaders and educators. Yes, Dewey led a revolution which has influenced us all. But for that revolution to be effective, for its consequences to be firmly based in American culture, there will have to be a good deal of dedicated effort in the days to come.

The school, however, is only one phase of education. Even if the Deweyan revolution here had been completely consummated, but no other institutions touched, it would be meaningless. For we are educated by all the institutions of our culture — language, the family, industry, politics — and the ways they function largely determine what we are. If freeing the possibilities that are in people for richly shared experience is the aim of education, then all institutions have to be pointed that way. Or the same thing follows if we turn the coin. To give youngsters the schooling that will help them to discover their best powers, only to let them loose in a society which frustrates their expression, is worse than stupid. It invites the social disaster which comes from resentment and pent-up hostilities.

What institutions should be changed, then, and how should they be changed? There is and can be no fixed, over-all plan. It is a matter of careful evaluation, of inquiry, of experiment. Dewey would ask: " Is a given institution, or system of human relations, affording sufficient opportunities for creative and shared experiences? If not, where and how is it falling short? How can it be made to function better as a means to desired ends? How are the ends themselves shaped by the means we use in attaining them? How can we best test whether a suggested improvement will fulfill its promise? " There are no easy ways to answer these questions. But methods of experimental science must be brought to bear on the relations of men, and when they are, they will probably be as fruitful of results as when applied to the relations of things.

For one thing, and almost as a first step, language has to be reconstructed. The words we use are freighted with the meanings of the dualistic tradition and often, instead of helping us, they stand in the way of dealing with our problems. So key words have to be redefined and, much more difficult, our minds have to be rechanneled in the process. From one point of view, all of Dewey's writings are simply the redefinition of such words as " experience," " knowledge," " mind," " truth," " logic," " intelligence," " means," " ends," " values," " education," " democracy," " freedom," " art," " religion." Ingrained as was the spirit of the professional philosopher in him, Dewey was nevertheless never concerned with this job for its own sake. The redefinitions, rather, are for the purpose of seeing more clearly, more accurately, the experiences to which the words point. And the need for this is better to see our human problems for what they are in the hope that, if we can once formulate them well enough, we shall devise means for better dealing with them.

So it is with knowledge. Knowledge, for Dewey, is a process of experiment, and ideas are indispensable tools, or instruments, in the process. Because of this conception, his philosophy has at times been labeled " experimentalism " and " instrumentalism." Ideas are instruments in the sense that they point the way to certain experiences. The ideas are true if they actually point that way, false if they do not; though for Dewey himself even this was not accurate enough, because of all the shadings and gradations in experience. He would have preferred to say that ideas are either more or less effective in pointing the way to the experiences we have in mind. Whether they are effective or not has somehow to be determined, and the most reliable way of determining this is by experiment. The method of controlled experimentation is science. And in so far as experiments warrant our continued use of an idea, we have knowledge.

But again, neither ideas nor knowledge are for their own sake, except as one experiences deep satisfaction in their possession. Their function in the ongoing scheme of things has to do with where they lead. Dewey has been so frequently misunderstood about this, by philosophers and laymen alike, that it is almost impossible to evaluate his influence; for one would have to distinguish between the influence of what he has incorrectly been thought to mean and the influence of what he has actually meant. A century or two from now, that distinction may be evident. Meanwhile, he is constantly assailed as believing that the practical is what pays off, that an idea is true if it works to our advantage, that success — financial, social, political, or whatever — is a person's crowning glory. William James once referred to the " bitch-goddess success " as a sign of his contempt for such " practical " materialism, but is to this day traduced for being just such a materialist. Exactly the same kind of thing has happened to Dewey. For anyone who understands him, it is obvious that a cash-and-carry sense of life is the enemy of everything he stood for.

When he says that ideas and knowledge are to be judged by where they lead, he means that we have to rely on them to bring us to the richest experiences we can undergo together. It makes sense, therefore, to make them as reliable as we can. Neither " practicality " nor " success " is what the human enterprise is all about. On the contrary, " shared experience is the greatest of human goods." To share with others the things that are most important and best for us has a deep quality afforded by no other experience in life.

But no one can tell another where the shoe pinches, or how and when the inner glow will come. We must be free to find that out for ourselves. To be sure, we stub our toes and sometimes break our necks in the process. Yet we grow by what we feed on, and the only diet fit for beings who would be human is one which permits us to stand on our own feet in our own ways, with self-respect and dignity enough to want that for everyone. To work with others for that kind of society is not merely the only path to its achievement; it is also part of the education we require to be able to live intelligently and maturely in such a world.

America is rich in its heritage, fortunate in its democratic roots and institutions. Democracy, however, is not something we have. Rather, it is a way of life to be attained; or, as Dewey himself said, it is a moral ideal. From the time of Roger Williams to the present, numberless men have labored and struggled to build a democratic community. In this twentieth century, put to the test as never before, we have had both giants and anonymous millions give everything they had to that task. Surely it does not belittle their contributions to say that, beyond all others in our time, one man has given body to the inspiration and the ways of achieving it, to the vision and technique of democracy. That man, of course, is John Dewey.

12

Franklin Delano Roosevelt

Bernard Bellush

Bernard Bellush is assistant professor of history at the College of the City of New York, and executive assistant in the extension division of the College. He is the author of *Franklin D. Roosevelt as Governor of New York*.

Franklin Delano Roosevelt

Bernard Bellush

Born of an economic stratum which knew little of the struggle and heartaches confronting the great mass of laboring men and women, Roosevelt the patrician was eventually hailed by many as their most ardent spokesman. It is ironic, also, that after having preserved the basic elements of our economy, Roosevelt should be denounced by so many as a traitor to his " class."

Franklin Delano Roosevelt was not a radical, and even less a Socialist as many have claimed. He did believe, however, that when our nation was confronted with a paralyzing crisis, such as the cataclysmic depression of the thirties, it was time to experiment, in hope of rescuing our nation's economic structure. For those who seek the key to his philosophy it is important to remember that Roosevelt was an active, spontaneous pragmatist. His consistency in seeking benefits for the people was, at times, hampered by his tactics and plans for specific legislation. One could almost hear Roosevelt saying to his advisers, " if this proposal does not work then let's try something else. But let's not sit back on our haunches lamenting that what was good enough for our grandfathers should be good enough for us."

When the National Recovery Act was shown to be a distinct failure in serving the great mass of people, besides being declared unconstitutional by the courts, Roosevelt showed his prompt willingness to set out on new paths by developing parity for the farmer, approving labor reforms which were long overdue, and devoting some much-needed attention to tenant farmers.

Roosevelt had the necessary characteristics to make of the presidency a vital, liberal, and energetic force. He had the power to handle men and the ability to recognize the potentialities of their experience and training for his own purpose. Thus, the brain trust. He institutionalized the "expertese" in government as early as his gubernatorial years. At times he made mistakes in the selection of advisers, but for the most part, he utilized their knowledge to good advantage and for the benefit of the nation as a whole. He had a keen sense of timing, trying to see through the eyes of the nation so as to interpret its needs, desires, aspirations, and fears. The one time he failed was with the court plan of 1937 when he misjudged the temper of the American people when tampering with long-held concepts and deep emotions concerning our judicial system.

As President, Roosevelt was the vital source of legislative suggestion, the final source of executive decision, the exponent of the nation's foreign policy, the representative of the nation and of its needs and interests, and the leader of his political party.

During the twelve years he served in the White House, Roosevelt fathered an extensive system of social-welfare legislation and modified many of our traditional attitudes. Today, his contributions are not merely an accepted part of the American fabric but are actively sponsored by his most ardent political critics. Not only did he preserve the best of our economic system but he played a dramatic role in revitalizing the people's faith, in themselves and in our government. In the process, Roosevelt did more than any other individual to thwart, if not permanently arrest, the radical movements of right and left.

The liberalism of his domestic program was not applied to American foreign policy during the early phases of totalitarian aggression in Europe and the Far East. However, with the realization by 1937 that Germany, Japan, and Italy would not be stopped short of war, Roosevelt thereafter took a strong and consistent stand against totalitarian imperialism.

Educators in particular owe a great debt of gratitude to Roosevelt. During the sixteen years he served as governor and as chief executive of our nation, he changed public opinion on the role of government, and in turn the role of the citizen in government. By his fireside chats and newspaper interviews he brought the presidency into the home of the voter and in an age of bigness and loneliness inculcated a feeling of closeness and of belonging on the part of the people toward their government.

One of the greatest tests a human being can face is physical incapacitation, especially on the part of a virile, active, and personable individual with obvious leadership qualities. Roosevelt overcame this tragic challenge during the years following his bout with infantile paralysis. Instead of isolating himself in the patrician environment of his Hyde Park estate, he eventually threw himself back into the political cauldron with as much fervor as he had previously exhibited as state legislator, Assistant Secretary of the Navy, and vice-presidential nominee. He successfully opposed the efforts of publisher William Randolph Hearst to capture the gubernatorial nomination from Al Smith in 1922. Two years later, with the assistance of crutches, a new Roosevelt brought some sunshine and hope to embattled delegates at the Democratic national convention with an inspiring nominating address for Smith. Four years later, Roosevelt again displayed leadership and inspirational qualities as he spoke up for the "Happy Warrior." Eleanor Roosevelt and Louis Howe had done their political homework quite well, so much so that FDR was on his way back to the political spotlight even sooner than he had dared expect.

Democratic delegates and party leaders at the New York State convention in 1928, finding themselves without an outstanding, eligible candidate willing to run for governor, drafted a reluctant FDR who was vacationing at Warm Springs, Georgia. Following a whirlwind campaign, election returns showed Smith defeated in his home state while FDR skimmed through victorious by a slim 25,000 vote plurality.

The four years Roosevelt served in Albany were, in essence, the genesis of the New Deal. During this period the bulk of the New

Deal program was discussed, formulated, or enacted in New York — housing, labor, prisons, agriculture, old age pensions, unemployment insurance, cheap and plentiful electric power, and effective regulation of utilities and of the sale of blue-sky securities. Many of the individuals who would play influential roles on the Washington scene received part of their apprenticeship with Roosevelt in Albany — Harry Hopkins, Frances Perkins, Henry Morgenthau, Jr., Raymond Moley, Thomas J. Parran, Jr., Leland Olds, Rexford G. Tugwell, Felix Frankfurter, Morris L. Cooke, James A. Farley, Eleanor Roosevelt, Samuel I. Rosenman, and others.

During his first gubernatorial campaign Roosevelt displayed a vigorous and unequivocal opposition to any form of racial or religious bigotry. He devoted many campaign addresses in the heart of the Ku Klux Klan region to denouncing the whispering campaign against Al Smith because of the latter's Catholicism. He also criticized those who might vote for him because of his opponent's Jewish affiliation. Few political figures on the contemporary scene had had the courage or independence of mind to take such a clear-cut stand on religious bigotry. Despite the ignoble treatment accorded the Japanese on the West Coast immediately after the outbreak of hostilities in 1941, Roosevelt was instrumental in developing an enlightened climate on the American scene which eventually insured the outlawing of racial segregation in our public school systems by the United States Supreme Court.

It is not sufficient to merely denounce such iniquitous practices as racial or religious segregation. What had to be done, and what Roosevelt did during a critical period in our nation's history, was to stimulate educational spade work through the establishment, for example, of the Fair Employment Practices Commission during World War II. Such measures helped lay a firm groundwork for significant advances in our culture during the last decade.

Prior to the calamitous depression which enveloped our nation like a thick smog, few political leaders dared state publicly that it was the definite responsibility of government to sustain and aid those who had become unemployed, sick, or incapacitated through no fault of their own. With too few exceptions leaders in American life believed that those who survived were the fittest and therefore it was not the responsibility of government but of private charity to look after the weak and incompetent. But even the laissez-faire, highly individualistic philosophy of President Herbert Hoover was undergoing a dramatic metamorphosis by 1932, for many of his policies were involving the Federal government in aiding increased numbers of unemployed workers and drought-stricken farmers. Although he moved hesitantly, with disturbed conscience and distraught spirit, Hoover was compelled to initiate, on a small scale, some badly needed changes. However, not until Roosevelt became President in March, 1933, did the Federal government assume a dynamic initiative in aiding the poor farmers, exploited factory workers, millions of unemployed, depressed youth, the aged, the sick, and the infirm.

Franklin D. Roosevelt was elected President by the " forgotten man " — the trade unionist, the man on relief, the small shopkeeper, the tenant farmer — all those who had experienced the emptiness of the prosperity of the 1920's. To the " forgotten man " the New Deal was also a symbol. It meant that the common man was to have his day of protection under the broadening arms of government. The New Deal extended the periphery of security from the businessman to include the farmer and laborer.

The New Deal comprised a galaxy of activities to meet the depressed conditions of American life: a general relief program, the Civilian Conservation Corps, the Home Owners Loan Corporation to save small property owners, a battle for a real public works program, farm relief, the National Recovery Act, a fiscal program which saved the banks, the Federal Deposit Insurance Corporation, the Securities and Exchange Commission, and the Tennessee Valley Authority. No single piece of legislation, or simple phraseology, can define the New Deal. It was an array of programs, a combination of attempts to solve major problems. Students will ever be perplexed by the variety, if not inconsistency, of some of these experiments.

During the first two years of his administration Roosevelt sought to reinstill in the people a note of confidence and hope for the future through the bright blue eagle banners of the National Recovery Administration. The business codes established by private enterprise under the NRA served to aid big industries and preserved the old strategy that government had utilized to revive the economy in previous years — by helping business one helps the nation. The positive aspect of NRA was section 7A — labor's first national bill of rights which had yet to be practically applied. The fundamental legislation which insured to labor a permanent and respectable standing in the community was the National Labor Relations Act and the Fair Labor Standards Act. These placed a ceiling over hours and a floor under wages. The Labor Relations Act, which was not in the strictest sense an administration measure, found Roosevelt's opposition of 1934 changing to support by 1935. This, however, was the only important piece of legislation of the New Deal period which Roosevelt had not initiated or at least advocated before its passage. But he supported it strongly once it passed and by 1936 was vigorously advocating minimum wage legislation.

With the assistance of such devoted individuals as Frances Perkins and John G. Winant, Roosevelt pushed through the Social Security Act of 1935. Not only did this legislation bring us abreast of western European nations, but workers learned that hereafter they would not starve if thrown out of work through no fault of their own; the elderly were to be aided by pensions, and the sick and incapacitated were to be succored. For the first time in the history of our nation the Federal government was directly involved in caring for its citizens.

Agreeing with proponents of public power development, FDR threw his support to the dream of Senator George W. Norris of the harnessing of the Tennessee River. The resulting Tennessee Valley Authority insured a revolution in the complexion and outlook of a seven-state area. President Hoover had opposed development of Muscle Shoals as a source of cheap electric power because it was a " socialistic " measure and a threat to the moral fibre of our nation. Roosevelt, on the other hand, was willing to experiment with this new proposal. He felt it would not only provide cheap and plentiful electric power, but would act as a yardstick, or catalyst, in stimulating private utilities to lower the exorbitant prices they charged consumers.

The residents of the seven southeastern states drained by the Tennessee and its tributaries had long suffered because of tragically low incomes. The prevailing poverty impelled thousands to flee the area, leaving Knoxville and other cities virtually ghost towns by 1932. Inadequate school systems, roads, and hospitals, and inferior governmental services characterized the area. Seasonal floods which came roaring down the Valley left deep scars of erosion on denuded hillsides.

Not many years after creation of the TVA and construction of huge, awe-inspiring multi-purpose dams, the rampaging floods were halted. Cows began grazing peacefully on hillsides, munching the newborn grass and producing milk for children who had seen little of it previously. Now regulated at a minimum depth twelve months of the year, the Tennessee began carrying hundreds of commerce-laden ships for many, many miles up the river. Factories grew up suddenly alongside, or near, the shores, while Knoxville and other centers surpassed their previous importance as thriving cities. A steady rise in tax collections insured improved school systems and modernized media of transportation and communication. The trend in migration was also reversed with the changes in the valley. Fishing, swimming, boating, scenic views, and resort areas now draw thousands of vacationers annually to this thriving, confident area which no longer suffers from an angry and uncontrolled river.

If Roosevelt had made no other contribution, the TVA was a sufficient and lasting memorial to his ingenuity, his faith in people, and his belief in the future. No matter what corner of the world where Americans may find themselves, one topic usually arises during a discussion with the interested and the alert of other countries — the TVA. They know of it and they have praised it in China, South Africa, Israel, Yugoslavia, and South America. Since its inception in 1933, TVA has been symbolic of the positive world leadership that the United States has played at times, and can play even more effectively in the future. The TVA, with its objectives and accomplishments, is one of our greatest weapons in the struggle for men's minds the world over.

When Roosevelt left Albany for Washington some twelve million unemployed had little hope for the future and a declining faith in themselves and in democracy. Private charities and local governments had exhausted their resources. Governor Roosevelt had made a serious effort, through the Temporary Emergency Relief Administration under Harry Hopkins, to provide work or home relief for the state's unemployed millions. Unfortunately, insufficient funds hampered the coverage and effectiveness of the TERA. Something had to be done, and done quickly.

As President, Roosevelt instituted a succession of administrative bureaus which all but taxed the alphabet — WPA, PWA, CCC, CWA, NYA, among others. Part of this work relief program put employables to work on slum clearance, rural electrification, and soil reclamation. Wages were paid on a security level — wages which were higher than relief payments but lower than those paid in competitive private enterprise — to win back the self-respect of individuals.

Some of those involved in work relief projects may have spent much of their time leaning against the sides of buildings, causing spectators to wonder whether the worker or the building was being held up. It may also be that some workers raked and re-raked the same leaves. But it should never be forgotten that the overwhelming number of men and women who secured work relief jobs were conscientious in their endeavors and left a permanent imprint on the face of our nation. Within the first two years of the Works Progress Administration there were constructed 1,634 school buildings; 3,000 tennis courts; 103 golf courses; 5,800 traveling libraries; and 1,654 medical and dental clinics. During this same period 128,000,000 school lunches were served; 1,500 theatrical productions were presented; and 17,000 literacy classes were given each month.

Playgrounds sprang up in the darkest corners of stifling, slum-stricken areas, giving children some room in which to flex their muscles and expend their energies in constructive endeavors. New post offices brought a fresh breath of beauty and confidence to cities and towns across the nation. The Civilian Conservation Corps took thousands of idle young men off street corners and away from incipient crime careers to help preserve the nation's natural resources and build hiking paths and shelters. But above all else, the CCC sought to retain the self-respect of our youth and their faith in democracy and in the future.

When hundreds of thousands of school-age youngsters were leaving school because of lack of sufficient funds at home, the nation was suddenly confronted with the possible loss of a generation of engineers, scientists, technicians, teachers, doctors, lawyers, and other professionals. Instead of continuing in the tradition of his predecessors, Roosevelt, in 1935, established the National Youth Administration which gave unemployed youth a chance in school, their turn as apprentices, and an opportunity for jobs and constructive careers through vocational guidance, training, and placement of apprentices. Within twelve months the NYA aided 600,000 youth. Before it concluded its work the NYA strengthened a generation of Americans against the inroads of totalitarian movements and insured responsible and competent men and women for the professions and for the industrial and economic worlds in time of peace and war. This was the generation which had been saved for our nation by the ingenuity and foresight of Franklin D. Roosevelt.

This product of a patrician environment was not a connoisseur of art, music, nor the drama. Yet, he felt that in time of crisis the nation must also help preserve the talents and self-respect of impoverished artists, musicians, writers, and dramatists. An unhappy, downtrodden, unemployed nation could not expect to produce significant cultural contributions. Roosevelt, therefore, sponsored projects which tapped the abilities of talented men and women for the pleasure and edification of their contemporaries and for the benefit of future generations.

With a philosophy based on overproduction, not undercon-sumption, Roosevelt sought to bring farm income up to parity with that of the worker in the city by restricting production, by soil conservation, by debt reduction and security against fore-closure, and by rural relief and rehabilitation of tenant and sub-marginal farmers. Before Roosevelt left the scene, the great mass of farmers were truly singing "Happy Days are Here Again."

One could go on and cite the efforts of Roosevelt to bring some semblance of order out of the stock market jungle, to pre-vent the sale of worthless securities, and of his attempt to insure stricter regulation of utilities for the benefit of the nation, through the formidable Securities and Exchange Commission. All this was done, or attempted, while Roosevelt was still able to concentrate on the domestic scene. With the passing years, how-ever, international developments loomed larger and larger on the American horizon. The growth of aggressive totalitarianism in Germany, Italy, and Japan paved the way for World War II and for the developing interest and involvement in international af-fairs by both the nation and its President.

From the vantage point of hindsight, an historian can see events and personal ties, causes and results, and from these factors boldly draw the main outline for recounting the errors and failings, the successes and victories of the past. The historian's advantage often serves as a handicap to those who played active, spontaneous roles at the time of the events. As interpreted by some historians, Roosevelt's was an inglorious role in foreign affairs. From the vantage point of elapsed time these historians expose certain weaknesses in his judgment and actions. Undoubtedly, all must agree that it was not within the power of the President to have prevented American participation in the war. More important, the thesis expressed by historian Charles A. Beard that Roosevelt knowingly and deviously led us into the conflict without consulting the American people has little genuine proof. If there is to be criticism of Roosevelt's role in foreign relations, it is that he did not commit the American nation and its military might to the cause of freedom soon enough. Intervention, in contrast to Beard's view, was too long delayed.

During his first term in office President Roosevelt pursued a rather narrow, if not nationalistic foreign policy, with the exception of relations with Latin America. It was in his first inaugural address that Roosevelt insisted: "In the field of world policy I would dedicate this Nation to the policy of the good neighbor — the neighbor who resolutely respects himself and, because he does so, respects the rights of others — the neighbor who respects his obligations and respects the sanctity of his agreements in and with a world of neighbors."

Carrying out this good neighbor concept, Roosevelt revoked the Platt Amendment ending our protectorate over Cuba, recalled our marines from Haiti, relinquished our treaty rights in Panama, and initiated a bold new precedent with personal participation in the 1936 Pan-American Conference. The Act of Havana, adopted at the 1940 meeting, was aimed specifically at the Axis powers for it warned that any outside interference in South America would be viewed by all members as an act of aggression and would be met with unity of action. The Monroe Doctrine had finally been broadened into a multilateral policy rather than the narrow, nationalistic approach of the nineteenth century.

Another policy which Roosevelt warmly supported and which contributed heavily to improving our relations abroad was the reciprocal trade program. The chief executive was granted power to reduce tariffs up to fifty per cent without the need for congressional approval. Sparked by the leadership of Cordell Hull, the executive agreements under this act afforded Roosevelt elasticity essential to building our international trade on a cooperative, friendly basis and of insuring mutual benefit to ourselves and to participating nations.

It was not long before world events began to shatter the illusions of many on foreign affairs. Despite Italy's brazen invasion of helpless Ethiopia in 1935, the American people, the President, and Congress clung tenaciously to the vain, if not naive, hope that we could isolate ourselves from foreign squabbles. Congress enacted the first in a series of neutrality measures granting the President the right to place embargoes on the export of material to belligerents and to deny them the right to raise funds in America.

The Spanish Civil War wrought havoc on the Iberian peninsula and opened the initial phases of World War II. To the chagrin and uneasiness of those liberals who rightly felt that the early years of the loyalist cause was the democratic struggle, Roosevelt responded with a policy of neutrality. In January, 1937, he requested an embargo on shipment of goods to both forces in Spain despite the fact that the duly constituted loyalist government was being challenged by insurgents who were openly supported by men, tanks, and planes from Fascist Italy and Nazi Germany. The battlefields of Spain served as a testing ground for the military equipment and strategy of the totalitarian powers.

Menacing clouds also hovered above the Far East, inciting new distress and fear. The Japanese, building their military might for an obvious invasion of the mainland, marched with daring ease across Manchuria and southeastern China. The impotence of the League of Nations in this crisis underscored its complete bankruptcy.

In his perceptive lectures delivered at the University of Chicago, George Kennan cautiously suggested that the causes of World War II had deeper roots than the immediate events in Ethiopia, Spain, and China. He felt that of greater significance, as in the case of Germany, was the fact that we Americans had failed in the 1920's, to give greater " understanding, support and encouragement to the moderate forces in the Weimar Republic." Had we done so, we might have thwarted the rise of Hitler.

When the Japanese initiated their full-scale offensive in China and shamelessly bombed helpless civilians in Nanking, and when Hitler's Germany marched into the Rhineland, President Roosevelt took a decisive stand against future totalitarian aggression. On October 5, 1937, he made clear that the aggressive designs of the Axis powers were imperiling the safety of the United States. With reserve and dignity he declared that as long as the present situation continued he would attempt to " quarantine " the aggressors. The American people, however, were still isolationist at heart, hoping that we might avoid embroilment in another conflict. Although, at the same time, we emotionally and actively cheered the allied cause, we refused to enter the European conflict until the Germans declared war upon us.

By 1938 FDR successfully requested a billion dollar naval expansion program. Before that dramatic year drew to a close, France and England agreed to the dismemberment of Czechoslovakia at Munich, hoping to satiate the whetted appetites of Hitler and Mussolini. Events moved swiftly within the next twelve months — Hitler marched into Czechoslovakia, took Memel, his partner sacked Albania, and then followed the attack on Poland. By September, 1939, World War II was officially launched.

With the tragic fall of France in 1940 FDR moved with speed and firmness, openly preparing the nation for inevitable participation in the struggle. Congress granted increased naval appropriations, accorded the President the right to call up the National Guard for active duty, and adopted the Selective Service Act. The President mobilized all of his executive power to aid Britain through release of fifty over-aged destroyers in return for leases to English possessions in the Western hemisphere. In July, 1940, Congress adopted the Export Control Act which gave the President the power to curtail or prohibit the movement of goods out of the country — an attempt to obstruct goods destined for Japan. By October, the President finally embargoed iron and steel scrap shipments to that country.

As part of his avowed policy in defense of Great Britain and the badgered western democracies, Roosevelt secured congressional adoption of Lend-Lease, insuring all-out aid to Britain, Greece, China, and the governments-in-exile. German invasion of the Soviet Union in 1941 meant a dramatic and fundamental change in the balance of power. Had both these totalitarian powers remained united, the western democracies might have had little, if any, chance of victory. The possibilities for freedom's success were augmented not only by this desired division but by the two-front battle the Germans had to wage.

The final entrance of the United States into the war was complete. Once involved in the conflict, the decisions taken under the pressure of war years were those of harassed, overburdened men, always performing under extremely harsh conditions — a factor which we, in retrospect, must try hard to remember. As George Kennan has so notably observed: " I think that some injustice is being done both to the men in question and to the cause of historical understanding by the latter-day interpretation which regards specific decisions of the wartime years as the source of all our present difficulties."

Our cooperation with the Russians during World War II

should not be viewed as a weakness in Roosevelt's foreign policy. It was a military necessity decreed by the exigencies of the conflict. The significance of the wartime conferences at Moscow, Teheran, and Yalta have perhaps been exaggerated. As revealed by the conference agreements, and by events of that time, the establishment of Soviet military might in eastern Europe and the entry of its forces into Manchuria was not exclusively the result of these discussions. Postwar Soviet control was primarily the result of Russian military operations during the final phases of the conflict. In addition, the arrangements at Yalta had the wholehearted support of the Chinese government. At least the democracies gave evidence of a sincere desire to establish friendly working relations with the Russians. These conferences serve as a permanent record of American hope for postwar peace. The events which followed exposed the brashness and insincerity of Russian motives.

In marked contrast to the conduct of the allies during the first World War, this second conflict was characterized by a high degree of cooperation among the united nations. The personal relationship between FDR and Churchill, usually without the formality of an ambassadorial intermediary, continued throughout the war, and eventually led to the inception of the United Nations. Throughout the war years Roosevelt stressed the need for, and facilitated, postwar planning among the allies. By June, 1944, he presented his administration's plans for an international organization. At Dumbarton Oaks the preliminary proposals were agreed upon. To win Russian cooperation at Yalta, Roosevelt and Churchill agreed that Byelorussia and the Ukraine be granted separate representation; that each member of the Security Council have the right of veto; and that the Soviet Union could annex eastern Poland. At San Francisco fifty nations gathered to approve the United Nations Charter shortly after the death of Roosevelt.

The significance of such an organization as the United Nations was always fully understood by FDR. Even in these days of troubled tensions and renewed pressures from totalitarian aggressiveness it stands as a positive and constructive monument to the high moral objectives of President Roosevelt. Perhaps we can criticize him for naively thinking that Russian cooperation could be counted on; perhaps we can chastise him for his simple faith in allied cooperation as a means of stemming future wars; but at least he left an organization through which nations can discuss and even diplomatically bargain for their rights and for future peace — for this we need not hush our praise. If the United Nations fails, it cannot be one individual who has failed us or even a few, but rather we the people who have failed to utilize the only possible instrument through which genuine peace and faith can be permanently restored to this world.

In a sense the New Deal was a revolution, for it revived hope and faith in American democracy and progressive capitalism at a time when the frontier of expansion seemed tightly closed forever by a devastating depression. The New Deal was also conservative and traditionally American for it preserved the best of our past, won support from all social classes by its aid to business, farm, and labor communities, and it stemmed the tide of socialism.

Franklin D. Roosevelt was a courageous leader of men and ideas. Yet he was a human being who undoubtedly made errors. He invigorated the American presidency, particularly in the field of foreign affairs, and strengthened popular institutions in the tradition of Thomas Jefferson, Andrew Jackson, Abraham Lincoln, Theodore Roosevelt, and Woodrow Wilson. He educated public opinion, leading it or following it as the occasion demanded. On the international scene he eventually repudiated isolation and fought successfully against the forces of totalitarian imperialism.

Index

A